SECOND EDITION

VOLUME SEVEN
Peggy Rathmann to William Steig

Favorite Children's
AUTHORS *and*
ILLUSTRATORS

E. Russell Primm III, Editor in Chief

ᴥ

PO Box 326, Chanhassen, MN 55317-0326
800/599-READ
http://www.childsworld.com

A NOTE TO OUR READERS:

The publication dates listed in each author's or illustrator's selected bibliography represent the date of first publication in the United States.

The editors have listed literary awards that were announced prior to August 2006.

Every effort has been made to contact copyright holders of material included in this reference work. If any errors or omissions have occurred, corrections will be made in future editions.

Photographs: 8, 36, 76, 140—Scholastic; 12, 60—Houghton Mifflin; 20, 48—Simon & Schuster; 40, 112—Hyperion Books; 44—Karen Hoyle / Kerlan Collection, University of Minnesota; 52—Carla Sachar / Farrar, Giroux, and Straus; 56—Graham Salisbury; 64—Pryde Brown / HarperCollins; 68, 108—Penguin Putnam; 80, 144, 152—HarperCollins; 84—Library of Congress; 88—Larry Meyer / HarperCollins; 92, 128—Harcourt; 96—Marc Simont; 100—Evan Cohen / HarperCollins; 116—Meredith Heuer / HarperCollins; 120—Random House; 124—Donald Sobol; 132—Houghton Mifflin / Kerlan Collection, University of Minnesota; 136—Peter Spier; 148—Kaiser Fine Photography / Suzanne Fischer Staples.

An Editorial Directions book

LIBRARY OF CONGRESS CATALOGING-IN-PUBLICATION DATA

Favorite children's authors and illustrators / E. Russell Primm III, editor-in-chief. — 2nd ed.
    v. cm.
  Includes bibliographical references and index.
  Contents: v. 1. Verna Aardema to Ashley Bryan.
  ISBN-13: 978-1-59187-057-9 (v.1 : alk. paper)
  ISBN-10: 1-59187-057-7 (v. 1 : alk. paper)
  ISBN-13: 978-1-59187-058-6 (v. 2 : alk. paper)
  ISBN-10: 1-59187-058-5 (v. 2 : alk. paper)
  ISBN-13: 978-1-59187-059-3 (v. 3 : alk. paper)
  ISBN-10: 1-59187-059-3 (v. 3 : alk. paper)
  ISBN-13: 978-1-59187-060-9 (v. 4 : alk. paper)
  ISBN-10: 1-59187-060-7 (v. 4 : alk. paper)
  ISBN-13: 978-1-59187-061-6 (v. 5 : alk. paper)
  ISBN-10: 1-59187-061-5 (v. 5 : alk. paper)
  ISBN-13: 978-1-59187-062-3 (v. 6 : alk. paper)
  ISBN-10: 1-59187-062-3 (v. 6 : alk. paper)
  ISBN-13: 978-1-59187-063-0 (v. 7 : alk. paper)
  ISBN-10: 1-59187-063-1 (v. 7 : alk. paper)
  ISBN-13: 978-1-59187-064-7 (v. 8 : alk. paper)
  ISBN-10: 1-59187-064-X (v. 8 : alk. paper)
  1. Children's literature—Bio-bibliography—Dictionaries—Juvenile literature. 2. Young adult literature Bio-bibliography—Dictionaries—Juvenile literature. 3. Illustrators—Biography—Dictionaries—Juvenile literature. 4. Children—Books and reading—Dictionaries—Juvenile literature. 5. Young Adults—Books and reading—Dictionaries—Juvenile literature. I. Primm, E. Russell, 1958–
  PN1009.A1F38 2007
  809'.8928203—dc22
  [B]   2006011358

First printing.

TABLE OF CONTENTS

MAJOR CHILDREN'S AUTHOR AND ILLUSTRATOR LITERARY AWARDS

THE AMERICAN BOOK AWARDS
Awarded from 1980 to 1983 in place of the National Book Award to give national recognition to achievement in several categories of children's literature

THE BOSTON GLOBE–HORN BOOK AWARDS
Established in 1967 by Horn Book *magazine and the* Boston Globe *newspaper to honor the year's best fiction, poetry, nonfiction, and picture books for children*

THE CALDECOTT MEDAL
Established in 1938 and presented by the Association for Library Service to Children division of the American Library Association to illustrators for the most distinguished picture book for children from the preceding year

THE CARNEGIE MEDAL
Established in 1936 and presented by the British Library Association for an outstanding book for children written in English

THE CARTER G. WOODSON BOOK AWARDS
Established in 1974 and presented by the National Council for the Social Studies for the most distinguished social science books appropriate for young readers that depict ethnicity in the United States

THE CORETTA SCOTT KING AWARDS
Established in 1970 in connection with the American Library Association to honor African American authors and illustrators whose books are deemed outstanding, educational, and inspirational

THE HANS CHRISTIAN ANDERSEN MEDAL
Established in 1956 by the International Board on Books for Young People to honor an author or illustrator, living at the time of nomination, whose complete works have made a lasting contribution to children's literature

THE KATE GREENAWAY MEDAL

Established by the Youth Libraries Group of the British Library Association in 1956 to honor illustrators of children's books published in the United Kingdom

THE LAURA INGALLS WILDER AWARD

Established by the Association for Library Service to Children division of the American Library Association in 1954 to honor an author or illustrator whose books, published in the United States, have made a substantial and lasting contribution to children's literature

THE MICHAEL L. PRINTZ AWARD

Established by the Young Adult Library Services division of the American Library Association in 2000 to honor literary excellence in young adult literature (fiction, nonfiction, poetry, or anthology)

THE NATIONAL BOOK AWARDS

Established in 1950 to give national recognition to achievement in fiction, nonfiction, poetry, and young people's literature

THE NEWBERY MEDAL

Established in 1922 and presented by the Association for Library Service to Children division of the American Library Association for the most distinguished contribution to children's literature in the preceding year

THE ORBIS PICTUS AWARD FOR OUTSTANDING NONFICTION

Established in 1990 by the National Council of Teachers of English to honor an outstanding informational book published in the preceding year

THE PURA BELPRÉ AWARD

Established in 1996 and cosponsored by the Association for Library Service to Children division of the American Library Association and the National Association to Promote Library Services to the Spanish Speaking to recognize a writer and illustrator of Latino or Latina background whose works affirm and celebrate the Latino experience

THE SCOTT O'DELL AWARD

Established in 1982 and presented by the O'Dell Award Committee to an American author who writes an outstanding tale of historical fiction for children or young adults that takes place in the New World

Peggy Rathmann

Born: March 4, 1953

When readers open up one of Peggy Rathmann's books, what do they find? They find bright, bold characters that pop off the page. They find stories that are fun and filled with color and humor. Rathmann is an author and illustrator of books for young children. There may not be a lot of words in her books, but Rathmann makes sure that each story is packed with plenty of excitement and action. Her eye-catching illustrations have won her the Caldecott Medal, the top honor for a children's book illustrator.

Margaret Crosby Rathmann was born on March 4, 1953, in Saint Paul, Minnesota. Every night, Peggy's mother and father would read to her and her two brothers and two sisters. Her parents tried to choose stories that appealed to all five children. Peggy especially loved Winnie-the-Pooh and Dr. Seuss stories.

SKIPPY, RATHMANN'S DOG, IS OFTEN IN TROUBLE. ONCE HE WAS VIDEOTAPED LICKING POACHED EGGS THAT WERE ABOUT TO BE SERVED FOR BREAKFAST. HE HAS ALSO EATEN WALLETS AND STOLEN DIRTY DIAPERS FROM THE DIAPER PAIL.

When Peggy started school, her favorite class was art. In seventh grade, she created some of her first pictures for display. When Peggy's brother was in high school, he ran for a seat on the student council. Peggy drew campaign posters for him. Her brother won the election, and students around the school took home the posters because they were so bright and creative.

As a child, Peggy also liked to write. At first, Peggy thought she might like to be a scientist, like her father. Part of being a scientist is making keen observations and writing them down. So Peggy began keeping a journal to document her days. She soon found, however,

A Selected Bibliography of Rathmann's Work

How Many Lambies on Grammy's Jammies? (2006)
Day the Babies Crawled Away (2003)
10 Minutes till Bedtime (1998)
Officer Buckle and Gloria (1995)
Good Night, Gorilla (1994)
Bootsie Barker Bites (1992)
Ruby the Copycat (1991)

Rathmann's Major Literary Awards

1996 Caldecott Medal
   Officer Buckle and Gloria

> *"There's a funny thing that happens between words and pictures. A picture book is a special medium because the pictures don't work without the words and the words don't work without the pictures. Pictures enable me to make a better story than I could with words alone."*

that it was much more fun to make up stories and tall tales than to write down the facts of each day.

When Rathmann was in college, she studied many different subjects. Although there were a lot of things she liked, she couldn't decide what she wanted to do for a job. Finally, she thought that she might like to teach sign language to gorillas. She took a course to learn sign language but soon learned that she would rather be drawing pictures of the gorillas. Rathmann immediately signed up for classes in writing and drawing for kids.

Many of Rathmann's characters are based on people she knows. Ruby from *Ruby the Copycat,* for example, is based on Rathmann herself. One of the main characters in *Officer Buckle and Gloria* was based on her naughty dog, Skippy. *Officer Buckle and Gloria* received the Caldecott Medal for its outstanding illustrations.

Rathmann knows that creating the perfect book for kids is hard work. Although *Good Night, Gorilla* has few words in it, the book took two years to complete. Rathmann changed the ending ten times until

---

RATHMANN'S NIECE SAYS THAT BOOTSIE BARKER, THE CURLY-HAIRED TERROR OF *BOOTSIE BARKER BITES,* LOOKS A LOT LIKE RATHMANN HERSELF.

she was finally happy with it. It was worth the
work, though. *Good Night, Gorilla* was honored
as a Notable Children's Book by the American
Library Association.

"All of my books have been based on embarrassing secrets."

Rathmann lives in San Francisco with
her husband. She likes to keep in touch with her audience. She travels
all around the country, reading to kids from her books and creating
drawings especially for them.

⚬

WHERE TO FIND OUT MORE ABOUT PEGGY RATHMANN

BOOKS

Rockman, Connie C., ed. *Eighth Book of Junior Authors and Illustrators.*
New York: H. W. Wilson Company, 2000.

Silvey, Anita, ed. *The Essential Guide to Children's Books and Their Creators.*
Boston: Houghton Mifflin Company, 2002.

WEB SITES

HAMSTERS
http://www.hamstertours.com/
To view Peggy Rathmann's Web site about hamsters

PEGGY RATHMANN HOME PAGE
http://www.peggyrathmann.com/
To read about Peggy Rathmann and her books

───

ONE OF THE FIRST BOOKS RATHMANN CREATED WAS
FOR HER NIECE. RATHMANN AND HER NIECE WERE THE STARS,
AND THEY WERE ATTRACTIVE, INTELLIGENT, AND POPULAR.

Margret Rey
H. A. Rey

Born: May 16, 1906   Died: December 21, 1996 (Margret)
Born: September 16, 1898   Died: August 26, 1977 (H. A.)

There are many wonderful animal characters in children's literature. One of the best-loved characters of all time is Curious George. The books featuring this lovable little monkey were written by Margret Rey. H. A. Rey, Margret's husband, illustrated the first seven Curious George books. More than 20 million Curious George books have been sold throughout the world.

Margret Rey was born on May 16, 1906, in Hamburg, Germany. Hans Augusto (H. A.) Rey was born on September 16, 1898, also in Hamburg. From 1927 to 1931, Margret Rey studied art at several schools in Germany.

AS A CHILD, H. A. REY SPENT MUCH OF HIS FREE TIME AT THE ZOO.
HE WOULD WATCH AND DRAW DIFFERENT ANIMALS.

She worked on her painting and drawing. She became a good artist. Her watercolor paintings were displayed in art shows in Berlin, Germany.

In 1930, Margret Rey got a job as a photographer. She first worked in Hamburg. Then, she moved on to work in London, England. In 1935, she moved to Rio de Janeiro, Brazil. She met and married H. A. shortly after arriving in Brazil. Margret and H. A. started the first advertising agency in Rio de Janeiro. They worked at their advertising agency before moving to Paris, France, in 1936.

In Paris, Margret Rey worked as a freelance writer. H. A. created illustrations for several French publications. The Reys decided to work together on creating children's books. Their first book, *How the Flying Fishes Came into Being,* was published in 1938. They published five other children's books before leaving France in 1940. These books were published in France and England.

> *"Among children we seem to be known best as the parents of Curious George, the little monkey hero of some of our books. 'I thought you were monkeys too,' said a little boy who had been eager to meet us, disappointment written all over his face."*
> —the Reys

The Reys left France during World War II (1939–1945). The German army was threatening to attack Paris. They first went to Lisbon, Portugal. Then they went to live in New York City.

CURIOUS GEORGE IS KNOWN BY DIFFERENT NAMES AROUND THE WORLD. IN ENGLAND, HE IS KNOWN AS "ZOZO," IN FRANCE HE IS CALLED "FIFI," AND HE IS CALLED "PETER PEDAL" IN DENMARK.

A Selected Bibliography of the Reys' Work

The Complete Adventures of Curious George (1995)
Curious George Goes to the Hospital (1966)
Curious George Learns the Alphabet (1963)
Curious George Flies a Kite (1958)
Curious George Gets a Medal (1957)
Curious George Rides a Bike (1952)
Billy's Picture (1948)
Curious George Takes a Job (1947)
Spotty (1945)
Pretzel (1944)
Cecily G. and the 9 Monkeys (1942)
Curious George (1941)
How the Flying Fishes Came into Being (1938)

One of the first books Margret Rey and H. A. created was *Raffy and the 9 Monkeys.* (It was published in the United States three years later as *Cecily G. and the 9 Monkeys.*) The Reys used one of the monkeys in this book to create Curious George. The first Curious George book was written before the couple left Paris. It was published in 1941, after they arrived in the United States. It was a very popular book. The Reys wrote

> *"He [Curious George] became very much a figure of his own. He knew what he could do and couldn't do. He became a person."*
> —*Margret Rey*

and illustrated seven Curious George books. They also wrote and illustrated several other children's books.

H. A. Rey died in 1977. After her husband's death, Margret Rey began teaching creative writing at Brandeis University in Massachusetts. She continued to work on the Curious George series. Rey served as editor for more than twenty-five additional Curious George books. She also helped to create the Curious George film series and movies for television.

Margret Rey died on December 21, 1996, in Cambridge, Massachusetts. She was ninety years old.

&

WHERE TO FIND OUT MORE ABOUT MARGRET AND H. A. REY

BOOKS

McElmeel, Sharron L. *100 Most Popular Picture Book Authors and Illustrators: Biographical Sketches and Bibliographies.* Englewood, Colo.: Libraries Unlimited, 2000.

Meister, Cari. *H. A. Rey.* Minneapolis: Abdo & Daughters, 2001.

WEB SITES

KIDSREADS.COM
http://www.kidsreads.com/series/series-curious-george.asp
To read a short biography of Margret and H. A. Rey

THE OFFICIAL CURIOUS GEORGE SITE
http://www.houghtonmifflinbooks.com/features/cgsite/
To find out everything about Curious George

MARGRET REY IS NOT CREDITED ON THE FIRST CURIOUS GEORGE TITLES.
LATER, THE REYS MADE IT CLEAR THAT THEY CREATED THE BOOKS TOGETHER.

Faith Ringgold

Born: October 8, 1930

African American history is an important part of Faith Ringgold's life. She uses her art and writing to tell the stories of her African American heritage. She is best known for the art and "story quilts" that she has created. She is also a successful author and illustrator of children's books. Her books include *Aunt Harriet's Underground Railroad in the Sky, Dinner at Aunt Connie's House,* and *My Dream of Martin Luther King.*

Faith Ringgold was born on October 8, 1930, in New York City. She grew up in a part of the city called Harlem. She loved the neighborhood where she lived. It felt like a small town because people were very friendly. Faith also liked to visit other parts of the city. Her childhood was an exciting time.

As a child, Faith suffered from asthma and often was sick. She had to stay home from school on many days. When she was at home, she listened to

THE TITLE OF RINGGOLD'S BOOK *TAR BEACH* COMES FROM HER CHILDHOOD.
SHE USED TO GO UP TO THE ROOF IN THE SUMMER TO COOL OFF.

jazz bands on the radio. She also filled her time by drawing. Her mother took her to art museums when she was healthy. These trips helped Faith decide that she wanted to be an artist.

After graduating from high school, Ringgold studied art at the City College of New York. Before she finished college, she married a jazz pianist and had two children, but the marriage did not last.

Ringgold then returned to college and after graduating took a teaching job in New York City's public schools. She worked as a teacher for several years.

When Ringgold's children were older, she took them on a trip to Europe. She wanted to see the great art that she had studied

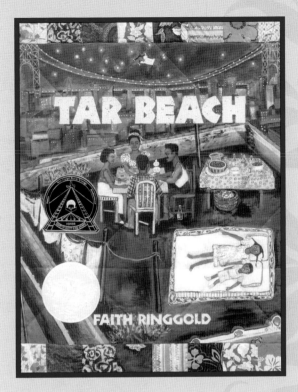

A Selected Bibliography of Ringgold's Work

Bronzeville Boys and Girls (Illustrations only, 2007)
Three Witches (Illustrations only, 2006)
Cassie's Word Quilt (2002)
Counting to Tar Beach (1999)
If a Bus Could Talk: The Story of Rosa Parks (1999)
The Invisible Princess (1999)
Bonjour, Lonnie (1996)
My Dream of Martin Luther King (1995)
Dinner at Aunt Connie's House (1993)
Aunt Harriet's Underground Railroad in the Sky (1992)
Tar Beach (1991)

Ringgold's Major Literary Awards

1992 Caldecott Honor Book
1992 Coretta Scott King Illustrator Award
   Tar Beach

as a student. When she returned to the United States, she decided to spend more time working on her art.

Faith Ringgold created paintings and other art in the next several years. Her artwork was exhibited at shows and galleries throughout the country. Before she died in 1981, Ringgold's mother liked to make quilts. She helped Ringgold re-create some of her paintings as quilts. Producing paintings as quilts instead of on canvas made them much easier to ship and carry around to galleries and exhibits.

Ringgold began to work on writing a story of her own life. People liked her quilts, but no one was interested in publishing her story. Ringgold decided to write her story on a quilt. These creations became known as "story quilts." She has created more than thirty story quilts since that time.

"I don't write sleepy-time stories—children don't really go to sleep reading my stories. I'd like for them to wake up and read my stories! But basically I want to inspire them to be all they can be and to know all they can know."

A children's book editor saw one of Ringgold's quilts. She asked Ringgold to write and illustrate a children's book based on the story from the quilt. Ringgold's first children's book, *Tar Beach,* was published in

IN THE EARLY 1970s, RINGGOLD HELPED START WOMEN STUDENTS AND ARTISTS FOR BLACK LIBERATION. THIS GROUP TRIES TO ENSURE THAT EXHIBITS OF WORK BY BLACK ARTISTS INCLUDE EQUAL NUMBERS OF PAINTINGS BY MEN AND BY WOMEN.

1991. Since then, she has written and illustrated several other books from her story quilts.

"I get inspiration from people. . . . When people are as good as they can be, I feel very inspired."

Ringgold continues to work on her art, her story quilts, and her children's books. She is also an art professor at a the University of California in San Diego. She lives in La Jolla, California, and also spends time at her art studio in New York City.

∾

WHERE TO FIND OUT MORE ABOUT FAITH RINGGOLD

BOOKS

Holton, Curlee Raven, and Faith Ringgold. *Faith Ringgold: A View from the Studio.* Boston: Bunker Hill Pub., 2004.

Kordich, Diane D. *Images of Commitment: Faith Ringgold.* Tuscon, Ariz.: Crizmac, 1994.

Ringgold, Faith. *Talking to Faith Ringgold.* New York: Crown, 1996.

Ringgold, Faith. *We Flew Over the Bridge: The Memoirs of Faith Ringgold.* Durham, N.C.: Duke University Press, 2005.

Turner, Robyn Montana. *Faith Ringgold.* Boston: Little, Brown & Co., 1993.

WEB SITE
FAITH RINGGOLD HOME PAGE
http://www.faithringgold.com/
To visit Faith Ringgold's own Web site, with biographical information

―――

RINGGOLD'S STORY QUILTS AND ART HAVE BEEN EXHIBITED IN THE UNITED STATES, EUROPE, SOUTH AMERICA, ASIA, AFRICA, AND THE MIDDLE EAST.

Willo Davis Roberts

Born: May 28, 1928
Died: November 19, 2004

Willo Davis Roberts never planned to write children's books! It really happened by accident. Today she is remembered as one of the best-known authors of children's mysteries. Some of her titles include *The View from the Cherry Tree, The Girl with the Silver Eyes,* and *Megan's Island.*

She was born Willo Davis on May 28, 1928, in Grand Rapids, Michigan. Her father had many jobs, often in different towns. The family moved a lot. In fourth grade, Willo attended six different schools.

Moving often was hard for Willo. It made it difficult to be successful in school. She wasn't in one place long enough to have good friends. One thing

ROBERTS WROTE MORE THAN THIRTY BOOKS FOR ADULTS
BEFORE PUBLISHING HER FIRST BOOK FOR YOUNG PEOPLE.

she was good at, though, was making up stories. Willo loved to read and write. "I began to write as soon as I could put the stories on paper; before that I just made them up and told them to my younger sisters."

In high school, Willo started writing a novel, but didn't finish it. After high school, Davis thought about whether to try a writing career. Five months later, she married David Roberts, a writer and photographer.

Willo Davis Roberts joined her husband in Oregon. For the next twenty years, she and David struggled with farming and raising their four children. Both of them worked hard at several jobs to earn a living. During that time, Roberts became successful at writing novels for adults.

"Mysteries were my favorite books to read when I was a child, so it was natural that when I began to write professionally I would turn to mystery/suspense."

A publisher told Roberts that one of her adult mysteries, *The View from the Cherry Tree,* might work better as a children's mystery. That publisher was right! It was an instant success.

Roberts wrote almost thirty books for young people. She enjoyed writing for children even though she thought it was harder than writing for adults. "I assume that my readers are intelligent, that they either know 'big' words or are willing to learn new ones. They are clever at figuring

---

BY THE TIME SHE WAS TEN, ROBERTS HAD READ ALL THE JUVENILE BOOKS IN TWO TOWN LIBRARIES.

A Selected Bibliography of Roberts's Work

One Left Behind (2006)

Blood on His Hands (2004)

Rebel (2003)

Undercurrents (2002)

Buddy Is a Stupid Name for a Girl (2001)

Hostage (2000)

The Kidnappers: A Mystery (1998)

Pawns (1998)

Secrets at Hidden Valley (1997)

Twisted Summer (1996)

The Absolutely True Story of My Visit to Yellowstone with the Terrible Rupes (1994)

Caught! (1994)

The View from the Cherry Tree (1994)

What Are We Going to Do about David? (1993)

Jo and the Bandit (1992)

Scared Stiff (1991)

To Grandmother's House We Go (1990)

Nightmare (1989)

What Could Go Wrong? (1989)

Megan's Island (1988)

Sugar Isn't Everything: A Support Book, in Fiction Form, for the Young Diabetic (1987)

The Magic Book (1986)

Baby-Sitting Is a Dangerous Job (1985)

Eddie and the Fairy Godpuppy (1984)

House of Fear (1983)

No Monsters in the Closet (1983)

The Pet-Sitting Peril (1983)

The Girl with the Silver Eyes (1980)

More Minden Curses (1980)

The Minden Curse (1978)

Don't Hurt Laurie! (1977)

The View from the Cherry Tree (1975)

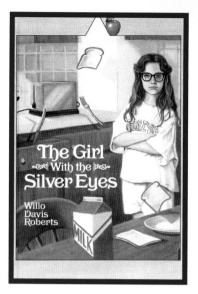

out plots, so I try to write ones that will keep them guessing," Roberts said.

Roberts liked to hook the reader right away. She liked the suspense to start as soon as possible. The ideas for her stories often came from her life, but as she wrote the story her imagination took over. Her stories are usually about young characters who are in a strange place or situation often without the help of adults.

Unexpected events occur, and the story is a puzzle. "These days many so-called mysteries are not mysteries at all, in the sense that you have a puzzle to solve,"

> *"Reading mysteries should be fun. Writing them certainly is!"*

remarked Roberts. But most important of all is the suspense. Roberts believed that "the reader must be kept in suspense, uncertain of the outcome, until the very last page, if possible."

Roberts enjoyed traveling around the United States with her husband and visiting classrooms to meet with her readers. She died of congestive heart failure in 2004 at the age of seventy-six.

∾

WHERE TO FIND OUT MORE ABOUT WILLO DAVIS ROBERTS

BOOK
Holtze, Sally Holmes, ed. *Fifth Book of Junior Authors & Illustrators.*
New York: H .W. Wilson Company, 1983.

WEB SITES
CHILDREN'S BOOK COUNCIL
http://www.cbcbooks.org/cbcmagazine/meet/wdroberts.html
To read a biography of Willo Davis Roberts

WILLO DAVIS ROBERTS HOME PAGE
http://www.willodavisroberts.com/
To read a biography and other information about the author

ROBERTS'S CHILDREN—AND NOW GRANDCHILDREN—ALSO
LOVE TO WRITE. HER CHILDREN HAVE ACTUALLY BEEN PUBLISHED.

Thomas Rockwell

Born: March 13, 1933

Thomas Rockwell read almost everything he could as a child. He read many kinds of books. He even read the information on cereal boxes. His love for reading and words continued when he became an adult. Rockwell has become one of the most popular authors of books for children and young people. His best-known books include *How to Eat Fried Worms, Tin Cans, Oatmeal Is Not for Mustaches,* and *How to Fight a Girl.*

Thomas Rockwell was born on March 13, 1933, in New Rochelle, New York. Writing, books, and art were important in his family. His mother was a writer, although none of her writing was published. She also read books to Thomas and his brothers.

Thomas's father was Norman Rockwell, the famous painter and illustrator. Many of Norman Rockwell's paintings of small-town life appeared on magazine covers. He was a very successful artist until his death in 1978.

ROCKWELL WAS CHOSEN AS THE BEST STUDENT IN HIS HIGH SCHOOL
CLASS OF TWENTY-THREE STUDENTS.

When Thomas was about five years old, the Rockwell family moved from New York to Vermont. Thomas loved the outdoors. He would spend many hours playing in the countryside.

Thomas did well in school, but he was often bored. As a high-school student, he was involved in many activities. He played basketball and baseball, and he was editor of the school yearbook.

After high school, Rockwell attended Princeton University. He stayed there for only two months and then transferred to Bard College. He majored in literature and wrote a lot of poetry. During his senior year of college, he married his wife, Gail.

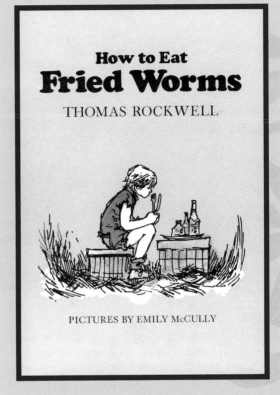

A Selected Bibliography of Rockwell's Work
How to Get Fabulously Rich (1990)
How to Fight a Girl (1987)
Oatmeal Is Not for Mustaches (1984)
Hey, Lover Boy (1981)
The Thief (1977)
Tin Cans (1975)
Hiding Out (1974)
The Portmanteau Book (1974)
How to Eat Fried Worms (1973)
The Neon Motorcycle (1973)
Squawwwk! (1972)
Humph! (1971)
Rackety-Bang and Other Verses (1969)

After graduating from college, he took a job in New York City as a writer for a gardening magazine. He left the magazine and moved to Upstate New York to help his father write his autobiography. Two books about Norman Rockwell's life and art, *My Adventures As an Illustrator* and *The Norman Rockwell Album,* were published in 1961.

"Just as I still haven't stopped reading the directions on cereal boxes and toothpaste tubes, so I don't suppose I'll stop writing."

After the books about his father were published, Rockwell struggled as a writer. He wrote a few short stories but was not sure what he would do.

Rockwell discovered his interest in writing children's books while reading nursery rhymes to his young son. He published his first book, *Rackety-Bang and Other Verses,* in 1969. Rockwell wrote another book of verses, but the publisher did not accept it. He went on to write several novels for children.

Rockwell's books include young characters who find themselves in crazy situations. He writes about serious issues but includes humor in his books. Young readers are attracted to his hilarious books even when the subject matter is unappetizing.

ROCKWELL COMES FROM A FAMILY OF ARTISTS. HIS OLDER BROTHER BECAME AN ARTIST AND HIS YOUNG BROTHER BECAME A SCULPTOR.

Rockwell continues to write for children and young people. He lives in Poughkeepsie, New York.

❧

WHERE TO FIND OUT MORE ABOUT THOMAS ROCKWELL

BOOKS
Holtze, Sally Holmes, ed. *Fifth Book of Junior Authors & Illustrators.*
New York: H .W. Wilson Company, 1983.

Something about the Author.
Vol. 70. Detroit: Gale Research, 1993.

WEB SITE
RANDOM HOUSE
http://www.randomhouse.com/catalog/display.pperl?isbn=9780440445456&view=excerpt
To read an excerpt from *How to Eat Fried Worms*

———

ROCKWELL'S BOOK *HOW TO EAT FRIED WORMS* IS ONE OF THE FIFTY
CHILDREN'S BOOKS MOST FREQUENTLY COMPLAINED ABOUT
IN SCHOOLS AND PUBLIC LIBRARIES.

Mary Rodgers

Born: January 11, 1931

Mary Rodgers is best known for *Freaky Friday*, her fantasy novel for young people. But she had never planned to be an author. A talented musician, she enjoyed a music career for much of her adult life.

Mary Rodgers was born in 1931 in New York City. Her mother was an interior decorator, and her father was the famous composer Richard Rodgers. He and his partner, Oscar Hammerstein, created many Broadway musical hits, such as *The Sound of Music* and *The King and I.*

Mary's parents sheltered her and her younger sister, Linda, from the show-business life. "I had a rather boring childhood," she recalls. "There were a lot of rules that . . . had to do with . . . when to go to bed and when to get up and what to wear and how to keep my room neat and how not to annoy my father."

To escape all the rules of her very orderly life, Mary spent hours reading. She also took music lessons for eight years. In her teens, she

---

IN 2003, *FREAKY FRIDAY* WAS MADE INTO A MOVIE FOR THE SECOND TIME.

wrote piano pieces and what she called "some very bad popular songs."

In 1948, Rodgers enrolled in Wellesley College in Wellesley, Massachusetts, majoring in music. She left college before graduation, though, to marry Julian Beaty. The couple had three children—Richard, Nina, and Constance—before divorcing in 1957.

Rodgers was involved in many music projects in the 1950s and 1960s. She and songwriter Sammy Kahn worked on song lyrics together. She also teamed up with conductor Leonard Bernstein to help produce the New York Philharmonic Orchestra's young people's concerts. Besides all these activities, Rodgers composed the music for several musicals. Her biggest success was the musical comedy *Once upon a Mattress*. It's based on the fairy tale "The Princess and the Pea." Opening in 1959, the show was a great hit with audiences.

In 1961, Rodgers married Henry Guettel, a motion picture company executive. They had two sons, Adam and Alexander. Over the next few years, Rodgers had her hands full with her music career and her five children. But she decided she wanted to write a children's book. Her

> *"Since I had nothing to do but take care of five children, a nine-room apartment, an eleven-room house in the country, and show up . . . eight times a month at the A&P [the local grocery store], I thought I'd be delighted to write a children's book, because I had all this extra time on my hands."*

BOTH RODGERS AND HER FATHER WERE NOMINATED FOR BEST COMPOSER IN THE 1960 TONY AWARDS FOR BROADWAY SHOWS. MARY'S MUSIC FOR *ONCE UPON A MATTRESS* LOST TO HER FATHER'S SCORE FOR *THE SOUND OF MUSIC*.

A Selected Bibliography of Rodgers's Work

Summer Switch (1982)
A Billion for Boris (1974)
Freaky Friday (1972)
The Rotten Book (1969)

picture book *The Rotten Book* was published in 1969. It's about a boy who imagines getting into lots of awful mischief.

Rodgers's best-known book, *Freaky Friday*, came out in 1972. It's about a teenage girl who wakes up one day to find she is in her mother's body. The book was so popular that Walt Disney Studios made it into a movie, which was released in 1977.

Rodgers followed up *Freaky Friday* with two sequels—*A Billion for Boris* and *Summer Switch*. Both are fantasy novels in which teens get involved in hilariously mixed-up situations. In 1984, *Summer Switch* was released as a movie, too.

Rodgers went on to serve on the boards of many arts organizations, including New York City's Juilliard School of Music and Lincoln Center for the Performing Arts. She currently lives in New York City.

❧

WHERE TO FIND OUT MORE ABOUT MARY RODGERS

BOOKS

Berger, Laura Standley, ed. *Twentieth-Century Children's Writers*. 4th ed. Detroit: St. James Press, 1995

Children's Literature Review. Vol. 20. Detroit: Gale, 1990.

Silvey, Anita, ed. *The Essential Guide to Children's Books and Their Creators*. Boston: Houghton Mifflin Company, 2002.

WEB SITES
MUSIC HELP WEB
http://www.musichelpweb.com/artists/rodgersm/rodgers.htm
For a brief biography of Mary Rodgers

THE RODGERS AND HAMMERSTEIN ORGANIZATION
http://www.rnh.com/org/index.php?page=biographies&person_id=133
To read a biography of this talented author, screenwriter, and composer

RODGERS AND HER MOTHER COAUTHORED THE BOOK *A WORD TO THE WIVES*. IN THE BOOK, THEY SHARED THEIR OPINIONS ABOUT RAISING A FAMILY IN NEW YORK CITY.

Eric Rohmann

Born: 1957

It's a good thing Eric Rohmann didn't leave the world of children's books. He thought about quitting before his book *My Friend Rabbit* came out. But children—and adults—loved it so much that he was convinced he should keep writing and illustrating.

Eric Rohmann was born in Riverside, Illinois, in 1957. He spent his childhood in Downers Grove, a suburb west of Chicago. Some of his hobbies included collecting rocks, insects, leaves, and animal skulls. Eric liked reading books by Maurice Sendak, Edgar Rice Burroughs, and J. R. R. Tolkien. Comic books were favorites, too. He also loved to draw monsters, knights, dinosaurs, and ships.

Eric was not a very good student. During classes, he drew space battles in his notebooks instead of paying attention. His high-school guidance counselor felt that Eric's best option was to pursue some kind of manual labor. He suggested, "[P]erhaps shipfitting or something in a lumberyard?"

ROHMANN SAYS THAT COMIC BOOKS TAUGHT HIM HOW TO TELL A STORY THROUGH PICTURES.

Fortunately, Eric did not follow his counselor's advice. Instead, he enrolled as an art major at Illinois State University in Normal. There he earned both a bachelor's degree and a master's degree in art. He went on to Arizona State University in Tempe, where he received a master of fine arts degree in print-making and fine bookmaking.

After college, Rohmann taught painting, printmaking, and bookmaking at Belvoir Terrace, an arts camp in Lenox, Massachusetts. He also taught at Saint Olaf College in North-field, Minnesota. Meanwhile, he continued to work on his own art. Sometimes he copied the work of artists he admired in order to learn from them.

A Selected Bibliography of Rohmann's Work

Clara and Asha (2005)
Pumpkinhead (2003)
My Friend Rabbit (2002)
The Prairie Train (Illustrations only, 1999)
The Cinder-Eyed Cats (1997)
King Crow (Illustrations only, 1995)
Time Flies (1994)

Rohmann's Major Literary Awards

2003 Caldecott Medal
   My Friend Rabbit
1995 Caldecott Honor Book
   Time Flies

> "Children are the best audience:
> they are curious, enthusiastic,
> impulsive, generous, and pleased
> by simple joys. They laugh easily
> at the ridiculous and are willing
> to believe the absurd."

Gradually, he arrived at a bold, colorful style that was truly his own.

Rohmann had always painted pictures that told a story. He began to realize that, if he strung several pictures together, they could become a book. In 1993, he gathered together samples of his work and went to New York City. There he visited several book publishers and showed them his pictures. Most of them sent him away.

Among Rohmann's work samples was a book idea about a bird that gets into a museum, enters a dinosaur skeleton, and goes back in time. After many rejections, this idea was finally accepted. It was published in 1994 as the wordless book *Time Flies*.

Rohmann's next self-illustrated book was *The Cinder-Eyed Cats*. It's about a boy who takes a magical sailboat to an island inhabited by cats with blazing eyes. Rohmann also illustrated a handful of books written by other authors.

Rohmann enjoyed illustrating children's books. But it was hard to earn a living as an illustrator, and he was thinking about giving it up. Luckily, he went ahead and published *My Friend Rabbit* in 2002.

AS A TEENAGER, ERIC ROHMANN WORKED AS A VOLUNTEER AT BROOKFIELD ZOO NEAR CHICAGO. HE ENJOYED FEEDING THE ANIMALS AND CLEANING THEIR CAGES.

> *"I've never known anybody like Rabbit [in* My Friend Rabbit*], but I've always, in some ways, wanted to be that carefree."*

In this story, Mouse shares his toy airplane with his friend Rabbit. This leads to havoc, but Rabbit has easy, breezy solutions to everything.

My Friend Rabbit was so popular that Rohmann decided to stay in the business after all. Today, he continues working from his home in a Chicago suburb.

❧

WHERE TO FIND OUT MORE ABOUT ERIC ROHMANN

BOOKS

Rockman, Connie C., ed. *Eighth Book of Junior Authors and Illustrators.* New York: H. W. Wilson Company, 2000.

WEB SITES

CHILDREN'S LIT MEET AUTHORS AND ILLUSTRATORS
http://www.childrenslit.com/f_rohmann.html
To read a biography and an interview of Eric Rohmann

HIS DARK MATERIALS [AN UNOFFICIAL FANSITE]
http://www.darkmaterials.com/rohm.htm
To see illustrations created by Eric Rohmann

THE LIBRARY OF CONGRESS NATIONAL BOOK FESTIVAL
http://www.loc.gov/bookfest/2003/rohmann.html
To read a short biography and watch a Webcast from the book festival

AS A BOY, ERIC ROHMANN ENJOYED PLAYING LITTLE LEAGUE BASEBALL IN THE SUMMER AND HOCKEY IN THE WINTER.

J. K. Rowling

Born: July 31, 1966

For the author of the incredibly popular Harry Potter fantasy series, life itself has been something of a fairy tale. In 1993, she was a single mother, wondering how she was going to feed her infant daughter. Four years later, she was the author of the best-selling series in the history of children's literature. This fairy-tale ending was the result of hard work and imagination, though, not of any wizard's spell.

Joanne Kathleen Rowling (pronounced "ROLL-ing") was born on July 31, 1966, in Bristol, England. Her father was an engineer at Rolls-Royce. Her mother was a stay-at-home mom, part French, part Scottish. They met during a train ride when they were both nineteen. Another fateful train ride, many years later, would change Rowling's life forever.

As a child, Joanne loved stories. She read books like *The Wind in the Willows* and C. S.

ROWLING ALWAYS CONCEIVED OF THE HARRY POTTER BOOKS AS A SEVEN-BOOK SERIES. SHE WROTE THE FINAL CHAPTER OF THE LAST BOOK MORE THAN TEN YEARS AGO. SHE RECENTLY PUT IT IN A VERY SAFE PLACE—ONLY SHE KNOWS WHERE!

Lewis's Narnia Chronicles. She began writing her stories at age six. Her first was about a rabbit named Rabbit.

Joanne's family moved several times while she was growing up. When she was nine, they moved from Winterbourne, England, to a country home in the Forest of Dean. Joanne and her younger sister, Di, loved hiking in the fields and playing games.

By the time she was a teenager, Joanne spent her lunchtimes telling stories to her friends—stories about their brave, heroic deeds. After graduating from Exeter University with a degree in French, Rowling moved to London and got a job as a secretary.

Rowling wrote short stories and worked on her unpublished novels in her spare time. On a train ride from Manchester to London in the summer of 1990, the idea for a story about a boy who was a wizard and didn't know it popped into her head. By the end of the trip, four hours later, she had come up with characters and a plot for the Harry Potter series.

> *"The books are really about the power of the imagination. What Harry is learning to do is to develop his full potential. Wizardry is just the analogy I use."*

In 1992, Rowling moved to Portugal to teach English. She married and had a daughter, but the marriage ended within a year. Rowling returned to England with her daughter to look for a teaching job. She

THE CHARACTER HERMIONE IS BASED ON ROWLING WHEN SHE WAS A YOUNG GIRL. LIKE THE CHARACTER, JOANNE WAS A HARDWORKING STUDENT WHO WAS A BIT ON THE PROPER SIDE AND A WORRIER.

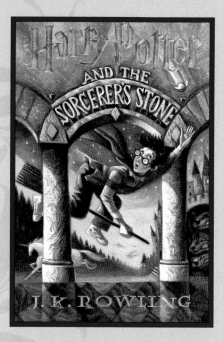

A Selected Bibliography of Rowling's Work

Harry Potter and the Half-Blood Prince (2005)
Harry Potter and the Order of the Phoenix (2003)
Fantastic Beasts and Where to Find Them (2001)
Quidditch through the Ages (2001)
Harry Potter and the Goblet of Fire (2000)
Harry Potter and the Prisoner of Azkaban (1999)
Harry Potter and the Chamber of Secrets (1999)
Harry Potter and the Sorcerer's Stone (1998)

worked on her story in cafés and coffee shops in her free time.

When she eventually finished, she sent it to publishers and received several rejections before it was finally bought. *Harry Potter and the Philosopher's Stone* was published in 1997. It was an instant hit!

The best-selling and award-winning book was released in the United States in 1998 under the title *Harry Potter and the Sorcerer's Stone.* It was an even bigger success in the United States, leading to the publication of five more titles. Rowling plans to write one more title for the series.

In 2001, the movie version of *Harry Potter and the Sorcerer's Stone* was released. It too was a huge hit. *Harry Potter and the*

Chamber of Secrets followed in 2002. Film versions of *Harry Potter and the Prisoner of Azkaban* (2004) and *Harry Potter and the Goblet of Fire* (2005) were also enormous successes. The fifth film, *Harry Potter and the Order of the Phoenix* will be released in 2007. Never imagining her success could reach the enormous height it has, J. K. Rowling is happy her writing has encouraged so many children to discover the joys of reading.

> *"People want life to be neat. . . . But life is not supposed to be neat. And it's a comfort . . . to all of us who have messed up. And then you find your way back, bizarrely."*

WHERE TO FIND OUT MORE ABOUT J. K. ROWLING

BOOKS

Beahm, George, *Muggles and Magic: J. K. Rowling and the Harry Potter Phenomenon.* Charlottesville, Va.: Hampton Roads Publishing, 2004.

Fraser, Lindsey. *Conversations with J. K. Rowling.* New York: Scholastic, 2001.

Gaines, Ann. *J. K. Rowling.* Bear, Del.: Mitchell Lane Publishers, 2002.

Ward, S. *Meet J. K. Rowling.* New York: PowerKids Press, 2001

WEB SITES
J. K. ROWLING HOME PAGE
www.jkrowling.co.uk
To find out all the latest information on J. K. Rowling and Harry Potter

---

A FAMILY NAMED POTTER LIVED FOUR DOORS AWAY FROM ROWLING WHEN SHE WAS GROWING UP. A COLLECTOR OF WORDS AND NAMES, ROWLING LOVED THE NAME POTTER AND DECIDED TO USE IT FOR HER MAIN CHARACTER.

Pam Muñoz Ryan

Born: December 25, 1951

Children of all ages enjoy Pam Muñoz Ryan's books. Her work ranges from cute picture books to engrossing novels for young adults. For many of her stories, she draws inspiration from her family background as a Hispanic American.

Pam Muñoz was born in Bakersfield, California, in 1951. She grew up in a multicultural family, with ancestors from Mexico, Spain, and Italy. Pam was the oldest of three sisters. Dozens of relatives lived nearby, too. They included aunts, uncles, grand-parents, and twenty-three cousins.

Pam's maternal grandmother used to tell her fascinating stories of her younger days. She had been forced to leave a life of luxury in Mexico and ended up in a U.S. camp for Mexican laborers. Pam's grandmother often

---

THE RYAN FAMILY HAS HAD MANY PETS OVER THE YEARS, INCLUDING DUCKS, LIZARDS, TROPICAL FISH, SNAKES, PARROTS, TURTLES, AND CANARIES. NOW THEY HAVE JUST TWO DOGS.

> *"I like to write because it's a job I can do in my slippers. That's a joke but in some ways it's true."*

spoke to her in Spanish, and that's how the girl learned her second language.

Summers were hot in the San Joaquin Valley where Pam lived. But the local library was air-conditioned, so Pam rode her bike there on sweltering afternoons. Partly, she wanted to cool off. But she also got hooked on reading and spent her days absorbed in the books she found.

With her active imagination, Pam spent hours daydreaming and pretending. She was a gracious queen, a

A Selected Bibliography of Ryan's Work

Nacho and Lolita (2005)
Becoming Naomi León (2004)
How Do You Raise a Raisin? (2003)
When Marian Sang (2002)
Mice and Beans (2001)
Esperanza Rising (2000)
Amelia and Eleanor Go for a Ride (1999)
Riding Freedom (1998)
California, Here We Come! (1997)
A Pinky Is a Baby Mouse (1997)
The Flag We Love (1996)
One Hundred Is a Family (1994)

Ryan's Major Literary Awards

2003 Orbis Pictus Award
  When Marian Sang
2002 Pura Belpré Award for Narrative
  Esperanza Rising

> *"I want to make sure children everywhere are excited about reading, so I visit schools and go to conferences to speak about reading and literacy. I want kids to be hooked on reading and books, like I was."*

bold explorer, or a heroic doctor. She liked putting on plays in her backyard, too. Pam was not too dreamy to work hard, though. When she was in elementary school, she often took jobs as a babysitter. In high school, she worked part-time in a department store.

She went to college at San Diego State University. After graduation, she became a bilingual teacher in Head Start, a program to help preschoolers from low-income families. She also married Jim Ryan, and they had four children. Then she went back to San Diego State to get a master's degree in education.

One day, one of her professors suggested that she write a book. According to Ryan, "That's when I discovered what I really wanted to do with my life." She started writing at age thirty-two, and her first children's book—*One Hundred Is a Family*—came out in 1994. It's a picture book that teaches counting by showing family members and family groups.

Ryan's first novel, *Riding Freedom*, is the story of Charlotte Parkhurst, who lived in America's Wild West of the 1800s. She disguised herself as a man because life was a lot easier for her that way. She eventually became a California stagecoach driver. Other notable

RYAN MAY REWRITE A STORY AS MANY AS THIRTY TIMES BEFORE IT'S PUBLISHED.

women appear in *Amelia and Eleanor Go for a Ride*. It relates true adventures of pilot Amelia Earhart and First Lady Eleanor Roosevelt.

Ryan's novel *Esperanza Rising* is a favorite for both young readers and adults. It's based on her grandmother's dreadful experiences as a young woman. Ryan decided to turn her grandmother's real-life tales into a novel.

Ryan wrote many delightful picture books, too. *A Pinky Is a Baby Mouse* teaches the correct names for baby animals. In *Mice and Beans*, some mice sneak up and take part in a little girl's birthday party.

Ryan is still at work in her home in Leucadia, California.

❧

WHERE TO FIND OUT MORE ABOUT PAM MUÑOZ RYAN

BOOKS

McElmeel, Sharron L. *Children's Authors and Illustrators Too Good to Miss: Biographical Sketches and Bibliographies*. Englewood, Colo: Libraries Unlimited, 2004.

Rockman, Connie C., ed. *Ninth Book of Junior Authors and Illustrators*. New York: H. W. Wilson Company, 2004.

WEB SITES

PAM MUÑOZ RYAN HOME PAGE
http://pammunozryan.com
To read Ryan's autobiography

READING IS FUNDAMENTAL
http://www.rif.org/readingplanet/bookzone/content/ryan.mspx
To read an interview with Pam Muñoz Ryan

———

SOME OF RYAN'S FAVORITE BOOKS AS A CHILD WERE THE LITTLE HOUSE ON THE PRAIRIE SERIES BY LAURA INGALLS WILDER AND *TREASURE ISLAND* BY ROBERT LOUIS STEVENSON.

Cynthia Rylant

Born: June 6, 1954

C ynthia Rylant did not think about being a writer when she was a child. She liked to read, but mostly she read comic books. Later, when she worked in a children's library, she discovered her love for books for children and young people. Since then, Rylant has become an award-winning children's book author. She has written picture books, short stories, novels, and poetry. Her best-known books include the

Henry and Mudge series, *A Blue-Eyed Daisy, A Fine White Dust*, and the Mr. Putter series.

Cynthia Rylant was born on June 6, 1954, in Hopewell, Virginia. Her parents divorced when she was about four years old. Cynthia and her mother moved to West Virginia, and Cynthia lived with her grandparents while her

RYLANT HAS WORKED AS A PROFESSOR OF ENGLISH
AT SEVERAL COLLEGES AND UNIVERSITIES.

mother attended nursing school. The house where she lived did not have electricity or running water. Cynthia and her mother moved to another small town in West Virginia when she was about eight years old.

Because her family was poor, Cynthia did not have many books to read. "I didn't do much reading because there just weren't that many books around," Rylant says. There was no public library in the town where she lived, but she could buy three comic books for a quarter. She would read them and then trade with her friends.

Cynthia's grandparents and mother did not talk about her father. She wondered about her father and wanted to learn

A Selected Bibliography of Rylant's Work

Alligator Boy (2007)

Ludie's Life (2006)

Boris (2005)

God Went to Beauty School (2004)

The Case of the Fidgety Fox (2003)

The Case of the Puzzling Possum (2002)

Henry's Puppy Mudge Takes a Bath (2001)

Poppleton (1997)

Mr. Putter and Tabby Walk the Dog (1994)

Missing May (1992)

Appalachia: The Voices of Sleeping Birds (1991)

A Couple of Kooks and Other Stories about Love (1990)

Children of Christmas: Stories for the Season (1987)

Henry and Mudge (1987)

A Fine White Dust (1986)

A Blue-Eyed Daisy (1985)

Miss Maggie (1983)

When I Was Young in the Mountains (1982)

Rylant's Major Literary Awards

2004 Boston Globe–Horn Book Fiction Honor Book
   God Went to Beauty School

1993 Newbery Medal
1992 Boston Globe–Horn Book Fiction Award
   Missing May

1991 Boston Globe–Horn Book Nonfiction Award
   Appalachia: The Voices of Sleeping Birds

1987 Newbery Honor Book
   A Fine White Dust

> *"I don't know why I became a writer. I didn't write much as a child. The only stories I ever tried were called 'My Adventures with the Beatles.' That was in sixth grade, when I was madly in love with Paul McCartney."*

about him. After several years, Cynthia's father contacted her. She dreamed of reuniting with him. Her dream did not come true, though, because her father died when Cynthia was thirteen years old. She wrote about her father and other childhood memories in her book *But I'll Be Back Again: An Album.*

When she finished high school, Rylant was not sure what she wanted to do. She attended college and discovered her love of writing in an English class. She finished college and found a job working in the children's section of the public library in Akron, Ohio. She spent much of her time reading children's books. She loved these books and decided that she would become a children's author. She also went on to receive a degree in library science and became a professional librarian.

Rylant's first book, *When I Was Young in the Mountains,* was published in 1982. It is a picture book about her life as a child in West Virginia. "So many of my books are

> *"Playing is still the greatest training you can have, I think, for being a writer. It helps you love life, it helps you relax, it helps you cook up interesting stuff in your head."*

RYLANT LOVED ANIMALS AS A CHILD. SHE STILL HAS MANY PETS AND OFTEN INCLUDES ANIMAL CHARACTERS IN HER STORIES.

directly connected to my real life, especially my childhood," Rylant says. She uses her writing as a way to remember her youth.

Rylant has published more than sixty books since 1982. She lives in Oregon with her son and their pets. She continues to write books for children and young people.

❧

WHERE TO FIND OUT MORE ABOUT CYNTHIA RYLANT

BOOKS

McElmeel, Sharron L. *100 Most Popular Children's Authors: Biographical Sketches and Bibliographies.* Englewood, Colo.: Libraries Unlimited, 1999.

Rylant, Cynthia, and Carlo Ontal. *Best Wishes.* Katonah, N.Y.: Richard C. Owen, 1992.

Rylant, Cynthia. *But I'll Be Back Again: An Album.* New York: Beech Tree Books, 1989.

WEB SITES

EDUCATIONAL PAPERBACK ASSOCIATION
http://edupaperback.org/showauth.cfm?authid=40
To read a biography of Cynthia Rylant

HARPERCHILDRENS
http://www.harperchildrens.com/hch/fiction/features/highrise/index.asp
To read an interview with characters from Cynthia Rylant's books

HOUGHTON MIFFLIN
http://www.eduplace.com/kids/hmr/mtai/rylant.html
To learn about Cynthia Rylant

KIDSREAD.COM
http://www.kidsreads.com/authors/au-rylant-cynthia.asp
To read autobiographical information by Cynthia Rylant

———

WHEN SHE WAS A YOUNG GIRL, CYNTHIA RYLANT DID NOT TRAVEL FAR FROM HOME BECAUSE HER FAMILY DID NOT HAVE A CAR.

Robert Sabuda

Born: March 8, 1965

Robert Sabuda has been called the Prince of Pop-Ups. With more than three dozen books to his credit, he is today's best-known pop-up book artist.

Robert James Sabuda was born in Michigan in 1965. He grew up in the small town of Pinckney in a little house by a lake. Books were an important part of the Sabuda household. Every evening before bedtime, his mother read a story to Robert, his older brother, and his younger sister.

Even as a child, Robert knew he was going to be an artist. He spent hours drawing, painting, cutting paper, and gluing things together. His bedroom, littered with art projects, was always messy.

Robert's father was a carpenter and bricklayer, and the boy loved watching him work. His mother ran Miss Judy's Dance School. Robert learned to

---

To SUPPORT HIMSELF AFTER COLLEGE, SABUDA WORKED AS A PACKAGE DESIGNER. HE DESIGNED BOXES THAT CONTAINED LADIES' UNDERWEAR.

tap dance there and, in the process, discovered how stories can be told through dance.

One day, Robert had to visit the dentist. He was a bit scared, so he picked up a book in the waiting room to distract himself. He opened it, and, as he recalls, "Something leapt right off the page. It was a pop-up book!"

"I don't ever recall a time that I didn't want to be an artist."

At once, Robert was hooked on pop-up books. People started giving him pop-ups as gifts, and he soon figured out how to make them himself. After many experiments, he proudly presented his mother with one of his artistic creations. It was Robert's own handmade version of *The Wizard of Oz*, by L. Frank Baum. In his words, it was "a pop-up book complete with cyclone!"

After high school, Sabuda enrolled in the Pratt Institute, an art school in New York City. While he was there, he worked as an intern at Dial Books for Young Readers. There he learned all about how children's books were produced. He also decided that he wanted to be a children's book illustrator.

"When being an artist is your job, you can make as many messes as you want to!"

After graduation in 1987, Sabuda showed his artwork to one publishing company after another. At first, he got a series of small illustrating jobs. Then in 1988, his first illustrated

WHEN SABUDA WAS A CHILD, READING WAS SO MUCH A PART OF HIS HOME LIFE THAT HE CANNOT EVEN REMEMBER LEARNING TO READ.

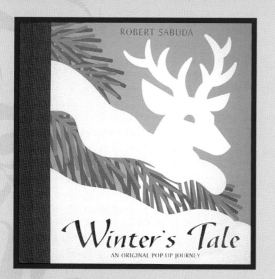

A Selected Bibliography of Sabuda's Work

Winter's Tale (2005)

Alice's Adventures in Wonderland (2003)

The Night before Christmas (2002)

Young Naturalist Pop-Up Handbook: Butterflies (2001)

The Wonderful Wizard of Oz: A Commemorative Pop-Up Book (With Matthew Reinhart, 2000)

The Blizzard's Robe (1999)

Cookie Count: A Tasty Pop-Up (1997)

A Christmas Alphabet (1994)

A Tree Place (1994)

Tutankhamen's Gift (1994)

Saint Valentine (1992)

Walden (Illustrations only, 1990)

The Fiddler's Son (Illustrations only, 1988)

The Wishing Well (Illustrations only, 1988)

Sabuda's Major Literary Awards

1994 Boston Globe–Horn Book Nonfiction Honor Book
  A Tree Place

books came out. They were *The Fiddler's Son* and *The Wishing Well*, both by Eugene Coco. In 1992, Sabuda published *Saint Valentine*. This was the first book that he both wrote and illustrated.

Sabuda still dreamed of publishing a pop-up book, and he finally got his chance. He wrote, designed, and illustrated his first pop-up book, *A Christmas Alphabet*, in 1994. With his pop-up passion unleashed, Sabuda went on to create more than twenty pop-up books. They bring mummies, knights, animals, dinosaurs, and many other subjects to life.

In 2000, Sabuda got to publish a professional version of his childhood Wizard of Oz project. It was *The Wonderful Wizard of Oz: A Commemorative Pop-Up Book*. The next year, he and his companion—writer and illustrator Matthew Reinhart—published two books in the Young Naturalist Pop-up Handbook series.

Sabuda is still making pop-ups today in his New York City studio.

Where to Find Out More About Robert Sabuda

Books

Rockman, Connie C., ed. *Ninth Book of Junior Authors and Illustrators.* New York: H. W. Wilson Company, 2005.

Silvey, Anita, ed. *The Essential Guide to Children's Books and Their Creators.* Boston: Houghton Mifflin Company, 2002.

Web Sites

KidsReads.com
http://www.kidsreads.com/authors/au-sabuda-robert.asp
For an interview with Sabuda

NPR
http://www.npr.org/templates/story/story.php?storyId=1534453
To listen to an interview with Sabuda

Robert Sabuda Home Page
http://www.robertsabuda.com/
To learn about Robert Sabuda, explore pop-ups, see a bibliography, and read about his contests

---

Sabuda says his favorite breakfast cereal is "piping hot oatmeal with butter and maple syrup!"

Louis Sachar

Born: March 20, 1954

Louis Sachar needs to be alone when he writes. He does not allow his family to be near him when he is writing—only his two dogs can watch. Sachar also does not talk about a book until he has finished writing it. He starts with a small idea and keeps working on the book until it is finished. Only then will he discuss it with other people. Sachar has written more than twenty books for children and young people. He is best known as the author of *Sideways Stories from Wayside School,* the Marvin Redpost series, and *Holes.*

Louis Sachar was born on March 20, 1954, in East Meadow, New York. Louis's family lived in East Meadow until he was about nine years old. His family then moved to Tustin, California. There were many

ALL THE CHARACTERS IN SACHAR'S BOOK *SIDEWAYS STORIES FROM WAYSIDE SCHOOL* ARE NAMED AFTER KIDS SACHAR KNEW WHEN HE WORKED AT AN ELEMENTARY SCHOOL.

orange groves near their house. Louis would walk through the orange groves on his way to school.

Louis was a good student in school. He liked math and played on a Little League baseball team. It was not until high school that Louis discovered his love of reading.

After he graduated from high school, he decided to attend a college in Ohio. He was there only a short time when his father died. Sachar was only eighteen years old. He returned to California to be near his mother. Instead of going back to college, Sachar worked for a few months. Then he went to college in California.

Sachar studied economics and was very interested in Russian literature. He studied Russian and took creative writing classes. Sachar also took a class that allowed him to work as a teacher's aide at a nearby elementary school.

> *"Writing for elementary school students, I've tried to recall what it felt like for me to be that age, because despite the notion that times have changed, I think that kids in grade school are basically the same as they were when I was young."*

> *"When I started writing, I spent a great deal of time alone. Solitude allowed me to think about a project at all times . . . and I was afraid that with someone else around, I'd lose valuable thinking time. But family life has given me a . . . stability which has improved my writing."*

AFTER PUBLISHING HIS FIRST FEW BOOKS, SACHAR WORKED ON HIS WRITING IN THE MORNINGS AND WORKED AS A LAWYER IN THE AFTERNOONS.

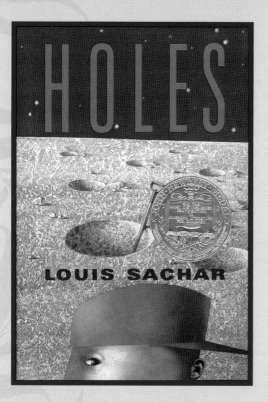

A Selected Bibliography of Sachar's Work

Small Steps (2006)

A Magic Crystal? (2000)

Marvin Redpost: Super Fast, Out of Control! (2000)

Holes (1998)

Wayside School Gets a Little Stranger (1995)

Marvin Redpost: Alone in His Teacher's House (1994)

Marvin Redpost: Is He a Girl? (1993)

Marvin Redpost: Why Pick on Me? (1993)

Marvin Redpost: Kidnapped at Birth? (1992)

Dogs Don't Tell Jokes (1991)

The Boy Who Lost His Face (1989)

Wayside School Is Falling Down (1989)

Sixth Grade Secrets (1987)

There's a Boy in the Girls Bathroom (1987)

Someday Angeline (1983)

Johnny's in the Basement (1981)

Sideways Stories from Wayside School (1978)

Sachar's Major Literary Awards

1999 Boston Globe–Horn Book Fiction Award
1998 National Book Award
1999 Newbery Medal
   Holes

After he was at the school for several months, Sachar was asked to be the playground supervisor at lunchtime. He played games with the kids. They called him "Louis, the Yard Teacher." Sachar used this name for a character in his first book.

When he finished college, Sachar took a job in a sweater factory in Connecticut. At night, he worked on his writing. He had an idea for a book about his experiences at the elementary school. He finished the book and sent it to many publishers. He also sent applications to law schools.

Sachar's first book, *Sideways Stories from Wayside School,* was published in 1978, during his first year at law school. Over the next several years, Sachar kept writing while attending school. He earned his law degree but decided to become a full-time writer.

Sachar lives in Austin, Texas, with his family. He continues to write books for children and young people.

ॐ

WHERE TO FIND OUT MORE ABOUT LOUIS SACHAR

BOOKS

McElmeel, Sharron L. *100 Most Popular Children's Authors: Biographical Sketches and Bibliographies.* Englewood, Colo.: Libraries Unlimited, 1999.

Silvey, Anita, ed. *The Essential Guide to Children's Books and Their Creators.* Boston: Houghton Mifflin Company, 2002.

Something about the Author. Vol. 104. Detroit: Gale Research, 1999.

WEB SITES

EDUCATIONAL PAPERBACK ASSOCIATION *http://edupaperback.org/showauth.cfm?authid=71* To read biographical information about Louis Sachar

LOUIS SACHAR HOME PAGE *http://www.louissachar.com* For biographical information and a list of works

ONE OF SACHAR'S DOGS, LUCKY, SEEMS TO UNDERSTAND THAT SACHAR WANTS TO BE ALONE WHEN HE IS WORKING. LUCKY GROWLS WHEN SOMEONE ELSE ENTERS THE ROOM WHILE SACHAR IS WRITING.

Graham Salisbury

Born: April 11, 1944

G raham Salisbury was not interested in reading as a child. "Embarrassing as it is to admit, especially to fellow writers, I didn't read until I was a little past thirty," says Salisbury. He read the books he was assigned in school, but he did not read for enjoyment. It was not until after his son was born that he began reading. Since then, he has grown to love reading. His love for reading got him started as a writer of children's books. Salisbury's books include *Blue Skin of the Sea: A Novel in Stories; Under the Blood-Red Sun;* and *Shark Bait.*

Graham Salisbury was born on April 11, 1944, in Philadelphia,

---

SALISBURY COMES FROM TWO FAMILIES THAT ARE DESCENDED FROM THE FIRST MISSIONARIES TO ARRIVE ON THE HAWAIIAN ISLANDS. BOTH OF HIS GREAT-GRANDFATHERS PLAYED AN IMPORTANT ROLE IN THE HISTORY OF HAWAII.

Pennsylvania. He spent most of his years growing up in Hawaii. Graham loved being a kid in Hawaii, where he spent many hours on the beach and surfing in the ocean. He would explore the forests and go fishing in the swamps. Graham spent most of his time having fun.

As a student, Graham attended a boarding school for grades seven through twelve. When he was in high school, he taught himself to play the guitar. He was very interested in music. "What I really wanted to be growing up was a rock and roll star," remembers Salisbury. After high school, he attended college in California.

When he finished college, Salisbury worked at many jobs.

A Selected Bibliography of Salisbury's Work
House of the Red Fish (2006)
Eyes of the Emperor (2005)
Island Boyz: Short Stories (2002)
Lord of the Deep (2001)
Jungle Dogs (1998)
Shark Bait (1997)
Under the Blood-Red Sun (1994)
Blue Skin of the Sea: A Novel in Stories (1992)

Salisbury's Major Literary Awards
2002 Boston Globe–Horn Book Fiction Award
    Lord of the Deep
1995 Scott O'Dell Award
    Under the Blood-Red Sun

> *"The important thing for me to understand as a writer for young readers is that though the world has changed, the basic needs of young people haven't. There are many, many kids out there with holes in their lives that they desperately want to fill. I can write about those holes."*

He was a teacher, a graphic designer, and a deckhand on a ship. He even worked as a musician for a short time.

After he was married and his son was born, Salisbury discovered his interest in writing. "Because reading eventually grew into something as large as life itself, I started feeling an urge to do some writing of my own," Salisbury says. He began writing many different things. He eventually realized that he enjoyed writing fiction the most.

Salisbury's first book for young people, *Blue Skin of the Sea: A Novel in Stories,* was published in 1992. This book, as well as others by Salisbury, is set in Hawaii. "I was raised in the Hawaiian Islands, a setting I know and a setting I love," Salisbury says. Writing about

> *"There are so many things to learn about writing— about thought, about feelings and passions, about storytelling, about craft, about commitment, and about one's own personality and habits. But in my mind, one element is most important. Without it a writer will struggle endlessly. That element is discipline."*

SALISBURY RECORDED AN ALBUM OF MUSIC UNDER THE NAME SANDY SALISBURY. HE ALSO RECORDED ALBUMS WITH A BAND CALLED MILLENNIUM. THE BAND ONCE HAD A NUMBER-ONE HIT SONG IN THE PHILIPPINES.

Hawaii allows Salisbury to remember his childhood. He is able to write about places that are important to him.

Family relationships are also an important part of Salisbury's books. "I was also raised—for the most part—without a father," Salisbury says. "I have some big holes in my life because of it. I'm reminded of these holes constantly, nearly every day of my life."

Salisbury lives in Portland, Oregon, with his family. Along with writing for young adults, Salisbury manages a historic building in downtown Portland.

⚬

WHERE TO FIND OUT MORE ABOUT GRAHAM SALISBURY

BOOKS

Rockman, Connie, ed. *Eighth Book of Junior Authors and Illustrators.*
New York: H. W. Wilson Company, 2000.

Something about the Author.
Vol. 108. Detroit: Gale Research, 2000.

WEB SITES

GRAHAM SALISBURY HOME PAGE
http://www.grahamsalisbury.com/
To read news about and a biography of Graham Salisbury

RANDOM HOUSE AUTHORS/ILLUSTRATORS
http://www.randomhouse.com/teachers/authors/results.pperl?authorid=26744
To read a Graham Salisbury biography and get fun facts

SALISBURY'S FATHER WAS IN THE U.S. NAVY AND WAS STATIONED AT PEARL HARBOR, HAWAII, ON DECEMBER 7, 1941, WHEN JAPAN ATTACKED. HE WAS KILLED IN WORLD WAR II (1939–1945) WHEN SALISBURY WAS ONE YEAR OLD.

Allen Say

Born: August 28, 1937

When he was only six, Allen Say decided to be a cartoonist. At twelve, he became an apprentice to the great Japanese cartoonist Noro Shinpei. Under Master Shinpei, Allen learned both to paint with a bamboo brush in the traditional Japanese style and to create Western-style drawings. The apprentice learned well. Allen's ability to combine East and West in a single drawing has made him one of the best-loved children's illustrators in the United States.

Allen Say was born on August 28, 1937. When he was a child, Allen lived in Yokohama, Japan. When he was only sixteen, he moved to California. He learned photography and decided to become a commercial artist. While working at a photographer's studio, Say finished illustrating his first children's book between photography assignments. For many years, he worked on his drawings for children in his spare time.

DURING WORLD WAR II (1939–1945), SAY ATTENDED SEVEN PRIMARY SCHOOLS WHILE TRYING TO AVOID THE BOMBS BEING DROPPED ON JAPAN.

Success came to Say when he began to create books based on his own life. The events in *The Bicycle Man,* published in 1982, came from his own childhood in Japan just after World War II (1939–1945). On spring sports day, the students at an elementary school are frightened when two American soldiers enter the schoolyard. Yet when one of the soldiers borrows a bicycle and performs stunts with it, fear turns to joy and laughter.

> *"I often go for walks to look for ideas. Ideas are what I call found objects. I can see them with the naked eye or visualize them in my mind. Finding ideas is a process of feeding one's mind with seemingly unrelated images and information. Then these things spark a thought or a progression of thoughts."*

Still, despite the success of *The Bicycle Man,* Say had doubts about whether he would keep illustrating books for children. When an editor asked him if he wanted to illustrate a story called *The Boy of the Three-Year Nap,* written by Dianne Snyder, he said no. The determined editor asked again and again until Say finally agreed. He decided that if he was going to illustrate one more children's book, he would do it exactly the way he wanted—the way he'd learned in Japan from Master Noro Shinpei.

Say locked himself in his studio and took out the old paint box he'd brought from Japan. When he began painting with his bamboo

THE INK-KEEPER'S APPRENTICE IS BASED ON SAY'S RELATIONSHIP WITH NORO SHINPEI, THE FAMOUS JAPANESE CARTOONIST WHO INSTRUCTED HIM WHEN HE WAS TWELVE YEARS OLD.

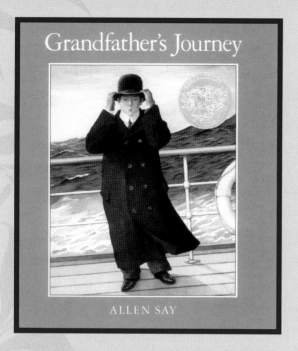

Grandfather's Journey

ALLEN SAY

A Selected Bibliography of Say's Work

Kamishibai Man (2005)
Music for Alice (2004)
Home of the Brave (2002)
Sign Painter (2000)
Tea with Milk (1999)
Allison (1997)
Under the Cherry Blossom Tree (1997)
Emma's Rug (1996)
Stranger in the Mirror (1995)
Grandfather's Journey (1993)
Tree of Cranes (1991)
El Chino (1990)
The Lost Lake (1989)
The Boy of the Three-Year Nap (Illustrations only, 1988)
A River Dream (1988)
How My Parents Learned to Eat (Illustrations only, 1984)
The Bicycle Man (1982)
The Ink-Keepers Apprentice (1979)

Say's Major Literary Awards

1994 Boston Globe–Horn Book Picture Book Award
1994 Caldecott Medal
   Grandfather's Journey

1989 Caldecott Honor Book
1988 Boston Globe–Horn Book Picture Book Award
   The Boy of the Three-Year Nap

brush, he discovered a new passion for his life's work.

After finishing *The Boy of the Three-Year Nap,* Say returned to writing and illustrating his own stories. In *Tree of Cranes,* a young Japanese boy listens to his American-born mother tell about the Christmases of her childhood. The son wants a Christmas tree for their Japanese home, and so his mother creates one—covered with silver origami cranes.

> *"At home, drawing really wasn't acceptable. My father, particularly, wanted a successful businessman for a son. So I drew, not in a closet, but always with a sense of guilt."*

In *Grandfather's Journey,* Say once again draws on his own life and the rich traditions of his Japanese ancestry. He tells the story of a man who—just like his own grandfather—comes to the United States yet never loses his Japanese ways. *Grandfather's Journey* won the Caldecott Medal.

Like his grandfather, Say has lived his life between two cultures. He has tried to work out the difficulties of belonging to both Japan and the United States—and yet also to neither country—in his drawings and paintings. Through his gentle storytelling, he helps young readers look into the hearts of people of different cultures.

❧

WHERE TO FIND OUT MORE ABOUT ALLEN SAY

BOOKS

Kovacs, Deborah, and James Preller. *Meet the Authors and Illustrators: 60 Creators of Favorite Children's Books Talk about Their Work.* Vol. 2. New York: Scholastic, 1993.

Something about the Author. Vol. 110. Detroit: Gale Research, 2000.

WEB SITES

EDUPLACE
http://www.eduplace.com/author/say/
For biographical information and an interview with Allen Say

WALTER LORRAINE BOOKS
http://www.houghtonmifflinbooks.com/catalog/authordetail.cfm?authorid=4430
To read a biography and see a photograph of Allen Say

———

WHEN HE WAS TWELVE, ALLEN SAY HAD HIS OWN APARTMENT! HE LIVED WITH HIS GRANDMOTHER, BUT THE TWO DIDN'T GET ALONG. SHE PAID FOR FOOD AND RENT SO THAT SAY COULD BE ON HIS OWN.

Alvin Schwartz

Born: April 25, 1927
Died: March 14, 1992

hildren love reading books of jokes and riddles. They also enjoy ghost stories. One author, Alvin Schwartz, became well-known for writing both kinds of books. He is also known for creating books

that tell the legends and customs, or folklore, of the American people. Some of his most popular books include *Tomfoolery: Trickery and Foolery with Words; Tales of Trickery from the Land of Spoof; In a Dark, Dark Room, and Other Scary Stories;* and *Flapdoodle, Pure Nonsense from American Folklore.*

Alvin Schwartz was born on April 25, 1927, in Brooklyn, New York. His family had come to the United States from Hungary and Russia in the early

SCARY STORIES TO TELL IN THE DARK WAS ONE OF THE MOST FREQUENTLY BANNED BOOKS BY SCHOOLS AND PUBLIC LIBRARIES IN THE EARLY **1990S.**

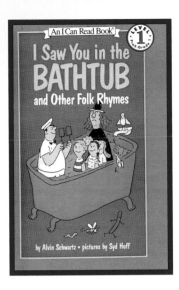

1900s. After settling in New York, they still held on to the customs from their culture in Hungary and Russia. They did not adopt the ways of most Americans.

As a result, Alvin grew up learning two ways of life. "I was affected by two cultures when I was growing up: the traditional beliefs and practices of my family and an American culture that had far less of an effect," he remembered.

A Selected Bibliography of Schwartz's Work

Stories to Tell a Cat (1992)

Ghosts! Ghostly Tales from Folklore (1991)

I Saw You in the Bathtub, and Other Folk Rhymes (1991)

Scary Stories 3: More Tales to Chill Your Bones (1991)

Gold and Silver, Silver and Gold: Tales of Hidden Treasure (1988)

All of Our Noses Are Here, and Other Noodle Tales (1985)

Tales of Trickery from the Land of Spoof (1985)

Fat Man in a Fur Coat, and Other Bear Stories (1984)

In a Dark, Dark Room, and Other Scary Stories (1984)

More Scary Stories to Tell in the Dark (1984)

Unriddling: All Sorts of Riddles to Puzzle Your Guessery (1983)

Busy Buzzing Bumblebees and Other Tongue Twisters (1982)

The Cat's Elbow and Other Secret Languages (1982)

There Is a Carrot in My Ear, and Other Noodle Tales (1982)

Scary Stories to Tell in the Dark (1981)

Flapdoodle, Pure Nonsense from American Folklore (1980)

Ten Copycats in a Boat, and Other Riddles (1980)

Chin Music: Tall Talk and Other Talk (1979)

Stores (1977)

Kickle Snifters and Other Fearsome Critters (1976)

Whoppers: Tall Tales and Other Lies (1975)

Cross Your Fingers, Spit in Your Hat; Superstitions and Other Beliefs (1974)

Tomfoolery: Trickery and Foolery with Words (1973)

Witcracks: Jokes and Jests from American Folklore (1973)

A Twister of Twists, a Tangler of Tongues: Tongue Twisters (1972)

Old Cities & New Towns; The Changing Face of the Nation (1968)

The People's Choice; The Story of Candidates, Campaigns, and Elections (1968)

Museum; The Story of America's Treasure Houses (1967)

The Night Workers (1966)

Alvin always knew that he wanted to be a writer. After high school, he went to college and studied journalism. After graduating from college, Schwartz went to work as a newspaper reporter from 1951 to 1955. Then, he worked as a writer and communications director for various organizations. During these years, he began writing books in his free time.

In 1963, Schwartz decided to devote most of his time to writing. He quit his regular job and turned a shed in his backyard into an office. His first books were nonfiction for children. The books were on social-studies topics such as government, cities, and the voting process.

"Exploring my national folklore has been a great and satisfying adventure."

In 1972, his book *A Twister of Twists, a Tangler of Tongues: Tongue Twisters* was published. It was popular right away. This collection of tongue twisters used humor and language that people enjoyed. It was also a collection of folklore. Schwartz had searched for tongue twisters in American culture. He decided to collect other types of folklore for his next books.

Schwartz went on to write many books of folklore. Each was popular for its humor, Schwartz's writing style, and the stories themselves. Some of the books had frightening characters that worried adults but thrilled children.

SCHWARTZ HAD FOUR CHILDREN—TWO BOYS AND TWO GIRLS.

Schwartz believed in the work he did. He believed it was important to share the stories of American culture. "Understand that you are part of a living tradition to which you contribute and from which you draw. You are deeply rooted in the experience of the human race and are part of something remarkable and continuous—the folk. At a time when everyone and everything seem in transit, it is good to know this," he stressed. Schwartz died on March 14, 1992.

> *"The folklore we create, pass on, and change says a good deal about us, about the times in which we live, and about the needs we have."*

WHERE TO FIND OUT MORE ABOUT ALVIN SCHWARTZ

BOOKS

Holtze, Sally Holmes, ed. *Fifth Book of Junior Authors & Illustrators.*
New York: H .W. Wilson Company, 1983.

Something about the Author.
Vol. 71. Detroit: Gale Research, 1993.

WEB SITES

HARPERCOLLINS
http://www.harperchildrens.com/teacher/catalog/author_xml.asp?authorID=12695
To read a short biography and list of works of Alvin Schwartz

---

SCHWARTZ WAS A MEMBER OF THE NATIONAL COUNCIL OF THE
BOY SCOUTS OF AMERICA FROM 1972 TO 1974.

Jon Scieszka

Born: September 8, 1954

on Scieszka gets his writing ideas from many different places. Many of them come from children—his own children, and the children who had him for a teacher. For example, some of the ideas that came from students in his math classes gave him the idea for his popular book *Math Curse.* Scieszka wrote this book hoping to help kids see that math can be fun. His Time Warp stories were the result of wondering what would happen if his students could travel through time.

FOR BREAKFAST SCIESZKA LIKES FRUIT AND A CUP OF COFFEE.
SOMETIMES HE STEALS HIS SON'S CEREAL OR PANCAKES!

Jon Scieszka was born on September 8, 1954, in Flint, Michigan. He grew up with five brothers. Jon's father was a teacher and then an elementary school principal, and his mother was a nurse.

After graduating from Albion College, Scieszka was accepted to medical school to become a doctor. But instead, he attended Columbia University to study writing. He wanted to write novels.

After finishing the writing program, Scieszka began teaching. He taught first and second grade. Scieszka had his students do a lot of reading and writing. He came to understand what interested the children. They made him think. Scieszka had always planned to write a novel, but working with his young students made him think about writing a children's story instead.

> *"What turns the ideas into stories and books is sitting down and writing, and rewriting, and throwing away writing, and writing some more. That's the hard part."*

While teaching, Scieszka met an author and illustrator named Lane Smith. They became friends. Scieszka and Smith decided to work together on ideas for a children's book. Although Scieszka enjoyed teaching and being with the children, he decided to take a leave from his teaching job for a year. During that year, he and Smith worked on their ideas.

THE TRUE STORY OF THE 3 LITTLE PIGS! IS TOLD BY
"A. WOLF." READERS LEARN FROM A. WOLF WHAT REALLY
HAPPENED DURING HIS ENCOUNTER WITH THE THREE LITTLE PIGS.

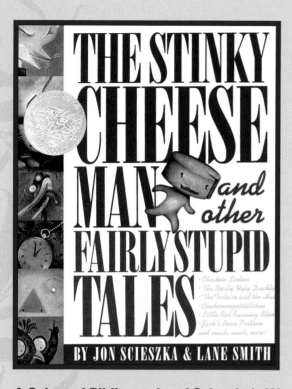

A Selected Bibliography of Scieszka's Work

Seen Art (2005)

Wild, Da Crazy, Da Vinci (2004)

Me Oh Maya! (2003)

Viking It and Liking It (2002)

Baloney, Henry P. (2001)

Sam Samurai (2001)

See You Later, Gladiator (2000)

It's All Greek to Me (1999)

Squids Will Be Squids: Fresh Morals, Beastly Fables (1998)

Summer Reading Is Killing Me! (1998)

Tut, Tut (1996)

Math Curse (1995)

2095 (1995)

The Book That Jack Wrote (1994)

Your Mother Was a Neanderthal (1993)

The Good, the Bad, and the Goofy (1992)

The Stinky Cheese Man and Other Fairly Stupid Tales (1992)

The Frog Prince, Continued (1991)

Knights of the Kitchen Table (1991)

The Not-So-Jolly Roger (1991)

The True Story of the 3 Little Pigs! (1989)

> *"I write books because I love to make kids laugh."*

Scieszka wrote the book *The True Story of the 3 Little Pigs!* during that year away from teaching. It was popular immediately. He has continued to write—or rewrite—well-known fairy tales. Some people think Scieszka's fairy tales are too difficult for children to understand and appreciate. But Scieszka knew that the twists in these "new" fairy tales would make children laugh.

Scieszka has written many books aimed at different readers. Some appeal to younger children. Others are especially appealing to boys. Scieszka tries to use language that kids would use and humor that they can appreciate.

Scieszka doesn't just write for children, though. He knows that readers of all ages enjoy the unexpected situations in his stories. He wants to tap into the intelligence of his readers, no matter what age they are.

Scieszka lives with his family in New York City. He continues to write books that fascinate readers with his offbeat style and humor.

❧

WHERE TO FIND OUT MORE ABOUT JON SCIESZKA

BOOKS

Berger, Laura Standley, ed. *Twentieth-Century Children's Writers*. 4th ed.
Detroit: St. James Press, 1995.

Marcus, Leonard S. *Side by Side: Five Favorite Picture-Book Teams Go to Work*.
New York: Walker, 2001.

WEB SITES

EDUCATIONAL PAPERBACK ASSOCIATION
http://edupaperback.org/showauth.cfm?authid=41
To read biographical information about Jon Scieszka, with
a book list and a summary of awards

THE NEW YORK PUBLIC LIBRARY: CHAT WITH JON SCIESZKA
http://kids.nypl.org/reading/SczieszkaChat.cfm
To get a book list for Jon Scieszka and read frequently asked questions from kids

BEFORE HE BECAME A WRITER, SCIESZKA SPENT
FIVE YEARS PAINTING APARTMENTS IN NEW YORK CITY.

George Selden

Born: May 14, 1929
Died: December 5, 1989

Chester Cricket, Harry Cat, and Tucker Mouse have delighted young readers for decades. They are the creation of George Selden, the author of seven popular books about friends helping friends. Known as the Cricket books, Selden's series about these three charming

animals has become a classic.

George Selden Thompson was born on May 14, 1929, in Hartford, Connecticut. His parents, Hartwell Green and Sigrid Johnson Thompson, raised their children in a home filled with books and music. When George was growing up, he developed a love of nature, which he later used as the setting for many of his books.

IN ADDITION TO WRITING BOOKS, SELDEN WAS
AN ARCHAEOLOGY BUFF AND AN OPERA LOVER.

In 1951, Selden graduated from Yale University with a bachelor's degree. That same year, he received a Fulbright fellowship to study at the University of Rome, Italy. After finishing his studies, Selden moved to New York City and started to write plays. But finding little success, he took the advice of a friend and experimented with writing children's books instead.

Selden's first book, *The Dog That Could Swim under Water: Memoirs of a Springer Spaniel,* was published in 1956. Selden never liked this book, and he was not disappointed when it went out of print. The following year, he completed *The Garden under the Sea,* a fanciful story

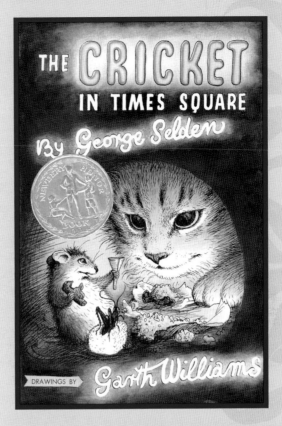

A Selected Bibliography of Selden's Work

The Old Meadow (1987)
Harry Kitten and Tucker Mouse (1986)
Chester Cricket's New Home (1983)
Chester Cricket's Pigeon Ride (1981)
Harry Cat's Pet Puppy (1974)
The Genie of Sutton Place (1973)
Tucker's Countryside (1969)
The Dunkard (1968)
The Cricket in Times Square (1960)
The Garden under the Sea (1957)
The Dog That Could Swim under Water: Memoirs of a Springer Spaniel (1956)

Selden's Major Literary Award

1961 Newbery Honor Book
  The Cricket in Times Square

about sea creatures living in Long Island Sound. These first two books set the stage for his famous Cricket books, which became the most successful writing of his career.

> *"My stories have to first please me. . . . I search for new ideas, am gratified when I find one, am nervous at the thought of putting even one down in words, and feel happiness when I think I've succeeded."*

Selden's first—and best-known—book in the series, *The Cricket in Times Square,* was published in 1960. Set in New York City, this animal tale depicts modern city life. A smart mouse, a kind cat, and a curious little boy become fast friends. They join forces to help a little country cricket survive in the city. Selden wrote six more books using the same three characters. Each of his books shares the same theme of friendship and loyalty and reflects his love for music, the Connecticut countryside, and New York City.

In addition to writing fiction, Selden also wrote nonfiction when subjects interested him. His fascination with the science of archaeology led him to write two biographies of scientists who discovered ancient places: *Heinrich Schliemann, Discoverer of Buried Treasure,* and *Sir Arthur Evans, Discoverer of Knossos.* He also wrote a play called *The Genie of Sutton Place,* which was later published as a children's book.

GEORGE SELDEN THOMPSON USED ONLY HIS FIRST TWO NAMES WHEN HE BEGAN TO WRITE BECAUSE THERE WAS ANOTHER WRITER NAMED GEORGE THOMPSON AT THE TIME.

Selden died on December 5, 1989, two years after publishing his final Chester Cricket story, *The Old Meadow.* Those charming tales hold a special place in children's literature. They are perhaps Selden's greatest contribution as a writer, for they show readers the importance of understanding and respecting differences. Above all, they demonstrate what it means to be a true and loyal friend.

❧

WHERE TO FIND OUT MORE ABOUT GEORGE SELDEN

BOOKS

Berger, Laura Standley, ed. *Twentieth-Century Children's Writers.* 4th ed. Detroit: St. James Press, 1995.

De Montreville, Doris, and Elizabeth D. Crawford, eds. *The Fourth Book of Junior Authors & Illustrators.* New York: H. W. Wilson Company, 1978.

WEB SITE

EDUCATIONAL PAPERBACK ASSOCIATION
http://edupaperback.org/showauth.cfm?authid=155
To read a biography of George Selden

———

SELDEN THOUGHT UP THE IDEA FOR HIS BOOK *THE CRICKET IN TIMES SQUARE* ONE NIGHT AFTER HEARING A CRICKET CHIRPING IN A NEW YORK CITY SUBWAY.

Brian Selznick

Born: July 14, 1966

Brian Selznick's books are easy to spot. His bold, detailed illustrations seem to jump right off the page. Selznick is also the author of many of the books he illustrates.

Brian Selznick was born in Perth Amboy, New Jersey, in 1966. As a child, he loved dinosaurs. When he was three or four, he used to visit his grandmother, and her maid gave him aluminum foil to play with. Brian used it to make dinosaur sculptures. He loved drawing, too, and monsters were favorite subjects. One of his kindergarten report cards said, "Brian is a good artist."

Brian's parents encouraged his art, and he took art classes after school. Sometimes he got in trouble for drawing monsters instead of doing his schoolwork. However, his fifth-grade teacher asked him to paint a mural,

---

SELZNICK'S GREAT-UNCLE, DAVID O. SELZNICK, WAS THE PRODUCER OF CLASSIC HOLLYWOOD MOVIES SUCH AS *GONE WITH THE WIND*.

> *"I love being an illustrator because I get to read really great stories, work with amazing people, travel and see places I never would've seen. And I get to draw all the time."*

or wall painting, in the classroom. Brian painted a giant green brontosaurus.

Brian hoped to become a set designer for stage shows. When it was time for college, he attended Rhode Island School of Design, an art school in Providence. His career plans changed after graduation, though, when he went to work in a children's bookstore.

For three years, Selznick worked at Eeyore's Books for Children in New York City. His duties included selling books, arranging the store's product displays, and painting big pictures on the windows. At first, he didn't know much about children's books, so his boss sent him home in the evenings with bags of them to read. This was when Selznick decided he wanted to illustrate children's books.

In 1991, while he was still working at the bookstore, Selznick wrote and illustrated his first book, *The Houdini Box*. It's about a boy who wants to imitate magician Harry Houdini's stunt of escaping from locked boxes. The book was a great success, and

> *"When you draw someone's face over and over again, you begin to feel a bit like you know them. . . . For a while it's as if they are back, sitting in your studio, whispering secrets in your ear."*

AMELIA AND ELEANOR GO FOR A RIDE WAS AN **ALA** NOTABLE CHILDREN'S BOOK AND A BOOK SENSE HONOR BOOK.

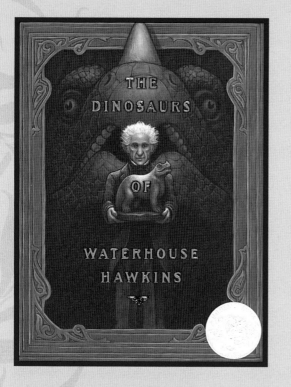

A Selected Bibliography of Selznick's Work

Rocket to the Moon (2007)

The Dulcimer Boy (Illustrations only, 2003)

The Meanest Doll in the World (Illustrations only, 2003)

When Marian Sang (Illustrations only, 2002)

The Dinosaurs of Waterhouse Hawkins (Illustrations only, 2001)

Barnyard Prayers (Illustrations only, 2000)

The Boy of a Thousand Faces (2000)

Amelia and Eleanor Go for a Ride (Illustrations only, 1999)

Frindle (Illustrations only, 1996)

The Houdini Box (1991)

Selznick's Major Literary Awards

2003 Orbis Pictus Award
   When Marian Sang

2002 Caldecott Honor Book
2002 Orbis Pictus Honor Book
   The Dinosaurs of Waterhouse Hawkins

Selznick soon quit his job to be a full-time illustrator.

Selznick went on to illustrate many books written by others, as well as books he wrote himself. He sometimes uses his books to explore his own childhood interests. *The Boy of a Thousand Faces* is about a child who loves old monster movies, just as Selznick did growing up.

Selznick often does extensive research before creating art for a book. For example, he was asked to illustrate *Amelia and Eleanor Go for a Ride* by Pam Muñoz Ryan. It's about the night in 1933 when aviator Amelia Earhart took First Lady Eleanor Roosevelt for a plane ride over Washington, D.C. To prepare, Selznick spent six months in Washington, D.C., doing research in libraries and museums. Selznick and Ryan also collaborated on *When Marian Sang*, about African American opera singer Marian Anderson.

Selznick indulged his love for dinosaurs in *The Dinosaurs of Waterhouse Hawkins* by Barbara Kerley. It's about the man who built the first life-size sculptures of dinosaurs in 1853. Selznick flew to London, England, and spent time in the park where Hawkins's sculptures stood. He photographed them, climbed on them, and drew pictures of them.

He currently lives in Brooklyn, New York.

&

WHERE TO FIND OUT MORE ABOUT BRIAN SELZNICK

BOOK
Rockman, Connie C., ed. *The Ninth Book of Junior Authors and Illustrators.*
New York: H. W. Wilson Company, 2004.

WEB SITES
BOOK SENSE
http://www.booksense.com/people/archive/selznick.jsp
To read an interview of Brian Selznick

CBC MAGAZINE
http://www.cbcbooks.org/cbcmagazine/dialogues/tracy-brian.html
For an author-editor dialogue

GRITS KIDZ BOOK CLUB
http://www.gritskidz.com/Interviews/ill_selznick.html
For an interview of Brian Selznick conducted by children

SELZNICK LIKES TO MAKE AND OPERATE PUPPETS. HE HAS PERFORMED IN AN UNDERWATER PUPPET SHOW AND IN A PUPPET BALLET.

Maurice Sendak

Born: June 10, 1928

Maurice Sendak has been a popular author and illustrator of children's books for more than fifty years. His best-known books are *Where the Wild Things Are* and the titles in the Little Bear series. He has also illustrated more than seventy books written by other authors.

Maurice Sendak was born on June 10, 1928, in Brooklyn, New York.

His parents were immigrants to the United States from Poland. As a young boy, Maurice's parents told him stories about life in Poland. These stories gave him many strong memories from his childhood.

Maurice's family moved many times when he was a boy, which made it difficult for him to make friends. A sickly child, Maurice spent much of his time indoors. He would look out the window to watch other children play. He drew pictures of people, houses, and other things he saw outside.

SENDAK OFTEN LISTENS TO CLASSICAL MUSIC COMPOSED BY WOLFGANG AMADEUS MOZART WHILE WRITING AND ILLUSTRATING HIS BOOKS. HE HAS MEMORIZED MANY OF MOZART'S COMPOSITIONS.

Maurice mostly read comic books, and he grew to love classical music. He also loved to go to the theater and watch movies.

When he was five years old, Maurice decided that he wanted to be an illustrator and author. He and his brother wrote stories and drew pictures on scraps of paper. Maurice's interest in drawing continued in school.

> *"The point of my books is to ask how children cope with a monumental problem that happened instantly and changed their lives forever, but they have to go on living. They cannot discuss this with anyone. No one will take the time. Parents are embarrassed so they'll shush them up."*

Maurice began his career as a professional illustrator while he was still in high school, working on the background art of several comic strips. He also wrote and drew his own comic strip for his high school newspaper. Several of his illustrations were included in a physics textbook written by one of his teachers.

Sendak's father wanted him to go to college after finishing high school. Sendak was tired of sitting in classrooms and was not interested in college. Instead, he took a job working in a warehouse. After two years, Sendak worked with his brother to design toys, which they tried to sell to a big toy store in New York City. The store did not buy the toys, but it did give Sendak a job designing window displays.

THE NAME SENDAK MEANS "FISH" IN POLISH. TO HONOR HIS FATHER,
SENDAK OFTEN INCLUDES A FISH IN THE SETS OF HIS THEATER PRODUCTIONS.

A Selected Bibliography of Sendak's Work

Mommy? (Illustrations only, 2006)

Swine Lake (Illustrations only, 1999)

The Miami Giant (Illustrations only, 1995)

Dear Mili: An Old Tale (Illustrations only, 1988)

Outside Over There (1981)

In the Night Kitchen (1970)

Where the Wild Things Are (1963)

One Was Johnny: A Counting Book (1962)

Little Bear's Visit (1961)

The Moon Jumpers (Illustrations only, 1959)

What Do You Say, Dear? (Illustrations only, 1958)

Little Bear (1957)

Kenny's Window (1956)

A Very Special House (Illustrations only, 1953)

A Hole Is to Dig (Illustrations only, 1952)

Sendak's Major Literary Awards

1983 Laura Ingalls Wilder Award

1982 Caldecott Honor Book
1982 National Book Award
1981 Boston Globe–Horn Book Picture Book Award
   Outside Over There

1971 Caldecott Honor Book
   In the Night Kitchen

1970 Hans Christian Andersen Medal for Illustrators

1964 Caldecott Medal
   Where the Wild Things Are

1963 Caldecott Honor Book
   Mr. Rabbit and the Lovely Present

1962 Caldecott Honor Book
   Little Bear's Visit

1960 Caldecott Honor Book
   The Moon Jumpers

1959 Caldecott Honor Book
   What Do You Say, Dear?

1954 Caldecott Honor Book
   A Very Special House

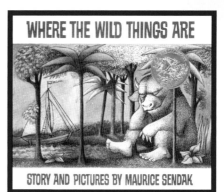

While he was working at the toy store, Sendak attended art school for a short time. He showed his drawings to publishing companies. Finally, he was asked to illustrate *A Hole Is to Dig,* a book written by Ruth Krauss. He continued to illustrate several books for other authors. *Kenny's Window* was the first book Sendak wrote and illustrated himself.

By the late 1970s, Sendak had become a famous author and illustrator of children's books. Along with working on his books, he began designing sets and costumes for theater productions. Sendak's love for classical music inspired him to work on several operas. He

> *"I have been doodling with ink and watercolor on paper all my life. It's my way of stirring up my imagination to see what I find hidden in my head. I call the results dream pictures, fantasy sketches and even brain-sharpening exercises."*

even adapted *Where the Wild Things Are* into a popular opera.

In 1990, Sendak cofounded The Night Kitchen, a national children's theater. He serves as the theater's artistic director. He lives on his farm in Connecticut, where he continues to write and illustrate children's books.

❧

WHERE TO FIND OUT MORE ABOUT MAURICE SENDAK

BOOKS

Gaines, Ann. *Maurice Sendak.* Bear, Del.: Mitchell Lane, 2001.

Sohnheim, Amy. *Maurice Sendak.* New York: Twayne, 1992.

Woods, Mae. *Maurice Sendak.* Minneapolis: Abdo & Daughters, 2001.

WEB SITE

KIDSREADS.COM: MAURICE SENDAK
http://www.kidsreads.com/authors/au-sendak-maurice.asp
To read an autobiographical sketch by Maurice Sendak and for further information

———

SENDAK WAS AWARDED THE NATIONAL MEDAL OF ARTS
IN 1996 BY PRESIDENT BILL CLINTON.

Dr. Seuss

Born: March 2, 1904
Died: September 24, 1991

Where would you find Dr. Derring's Singing Herrings, Plain-Belly Sneetches, or Floob-Boober-Bab-Boober-Bubs? These and many other strange and interesting characters can be found only in the books written by Dr. Seuss.

Dr. Seuss's real name was Theodore Seuss Geisel. (He also wrote books using the name Theo LeSieg, which is Geisel spelled backward.) He was born on March 2, 1904, in Springfield, Massachusetts. As a young boy, Theodore discovered that he loved to draw funny characters and write humorous stories.

DR. SEUSS WAS AWARDED AN HONORARY PULITZER PRIZE IN 1984 FOR HIS HALF CENTURY OF CONTRIBUTIONS TO "THE EDUCATION AND ENJOYMENT OF AMERICA'S CHILDREN AND THEIR PARENTS."

When he was a student at Dartmouth College in Hanover, New Hampshire, Geisel worked on the college humor magazine. He edited and contributed cartoons and stories to it. It was in this role that he started to refer to himself as "Seuss."

From his early days as a writer, Geisel used rhythm in his writing. His first children's book, *And to Think That I Saw It on Mulberry Street,* was a kind of poem written to the rhythm of a ship's engine. It was the start of a long career in children's books!

Geisel was challenged to write more children's books after examining a report about how children learn to read. The report said that many children's readers

A Selected Bibliography of Dr. Seuss's Work

The Big Brag (1986)
The Butter Battle Book (1984)
The Lorax (1971)
Fox in Socks (1965)
Dr. Seuss's ABC (1963)
Hop on Pop (1963)
Green Eggs and Ham (1960)
One Fish, Two Fish, Red Fish, Blue Fish (1960)
Yertle the Turtle and Other Stories (1958)
The Cat in the Hat (1957)
How the Grinch Stole Christmas (1957)
If I Ran the Circus (1956)
Horton Hears a Who! (1954)
If I Ran the Zoo (1950)
Bartholomew and the Oobleck (1949)
McElligot's Pool (1947)
Horton Hatches the Egg (1940)
The 500 Hats of Bartholomew Cubbins (1938)
And to Think That I Saw it On Mulberry Street (1938)

Dr. Seuss's Major Literary Awards

1980 Laura Ingalls Wilder Award
1951 Caldecott Honor Book
    If I Ran the Zoo
1950 Caldecott Honor Book
    Bartholomew and the Oobleck
1948 Caldecott Honor Book
    McElligot's Pool

were not interesting to young people. Geisel decided to write a children's book that would be simple and fun for kids to read. He called his book *The Cat in the Hat.* It went on to be one of Dr. Seuss's most famous books. In this book and most others that he wrote, Dr. Seuss included a list of vocabulary words.

> *"[Dr. Seuss's first children's book] was finally accepted when an old Dartmouth friend who had become a children's book publisher . . . bumped into me on the street. See, everything has to do with luck."*

Dr. Seuss believed that it was important to have illustrations in his books to help tell the story and entertain the reader. He created many bizarre animals and characters including Foo-Foo the Snoo, the Lorax, and Single-File Zummzian Zuks.

In his writing, Dr. Seuss used rhyming words. He believed that rhyme helped children read and make reading more fun. He also created his own words by using parts of different words and sounds. Dr. Seuss often used his funny characters to tell stories about serious issues.

Dr. Seuss won three Academy Awards in his career. The first was in 1947 for a script he wrote during World War II (1939–1945) called *Design for Death,* a documentary about the Japanese people. The second was for best documentary short subject film in 1946—*Your Job in*

IN 2000, *HOW THE GRINCH STOLE CHRISTMAS* WAS MADE INTO A MOTION PICTURE STARRING JIM CARREY.

Germany, or *Hitler Lives*. His third Academy Award was in 1951 for the cartoon *Gerald McBoing-Boing*.

Many of Dr. Seuss's books were made into television shows for children. Dr. Seuss died on September 24, 1991, at the age of eighty-seven. At the time of this death, some 200 million Dr. Seuss books had been sold around the world.

&

WHERE TO FIND OUT MORE ABOUT DR. SEUSS

BOOKS

Geisel, Audrey. *The Secret Art of Dr. Seuss*. New York: Random House, 1995.

Morgan, Judith, and Neil Morgan. *Dr. Seuss and Mr. Geisel: A Biography*. New York: Da Capo Press, 1996.

Weidt, Maryann N. *Oh, the Places He Went: A Story about Dr. Seuss–Theodor Seuss Geisel*. Minneapolis: Carolrhoda, 1995.

WEB SITES

THE DR. SEUSS HOME PAGE
http://www.seuss.org/
To read a biographical sketch of Dr. Seuss, to get information about his books, and to find out details about famous Dr. Seuss videos

WELCOME TO SEUSSVILLE
http://www.randomhouse.com/seussville/
To go on an interactive tour of Dr. Seuss's world that includes biographical information about the author, details about his books, and descriptions of his characters

—

SIX DR. SEUSS BOOKS WERE PRODUCED AFTER HIS DEATH IN 1991. THEY WERE BASED ON REMAINING DR. SEUSS MATERIALS AND, IN ONE CASE, A MANUSCRIPT.

Shel Silverstein

Born: September 25, 1930
Died: May 8, 1999

Shel Silverstein was a man of many talents. He wrote songs, plays, and books for adults and children. He drew cartoons and illustrations for books and magazines. He is best known as a children's book author. His most popular children's books are *The Giving Tree; Where the Sidewalk Ends: The Poems & Drawings of Shel Silverstein;* and *A Light in the Attic.*

Shel Silverstein was born on September 25, 1930, in Chicago, Illinois. As a young boy, Shel wanted to be a baseball player. He was not a very good player, though, so he knew he would not become a pro. He spent much of his time

---

IN 1984, SILVERSTEIN WON A GRAMMY AWARD FOR THE
RECORDING OF HIS POETRY COLLECTION *WHERE THE SIDEWALK ENDS.*

drawing and writing instead. He learned to draw and became a talented cartoonist as a young man.

When he finished high school in the early 1950s, Silverstein joined the U.S. Army. He was stationed in Korea and Japan. People in the military recognized Silverstein's talent for drawing and cartooning. He was assigned to be a cartoonist for the Pacific *Stars and Stripes,* a newspaper published by the U.S. military.

When he left the army, Silverstein got a job as a writer and cartoonist for a magazine for adults. Many of his cartoons and humorous drawings from the magazine were published in a book collection. Along with drawing, he also began writing songs. Many of his songs were recorded by country music artists. One of his songs, "A Boy Named Sue," was recorded by Johnny Cash and became a number-one hit.

Silverstein's career was going very well. He did not plan to write or illustrate books for children until a friend introduced him to a children's book editor. The editor convinced Silverstein that he should create a children's book.

> *"When I was a kid—twelve, fourteen, around there—I would much rather have been a good baseball player or a hit with the girls. But I couldn't play ball; I couldn't dance. Luckily, the girls didn't want me. . . . So, I started to draw and to write."*

SILVERSTEIN COMPOSED THE MUSIC FOR THE MOVIE *POSTCARDS FROM THE EDGE.* HE RECEIVED AN ACADEMY AWARD NOMINATION FOR A SONG USED IN THE MOVIE.

A Selected Bibliography of Silverstein's Work

Falling Up: Poems and Drawings (1996)

A Light in the Attic (1981)

The Missing Piece Meets the Big O (1981)

The Missing Piece (1976)

Where the Sidewalk Ends: The Poems & Drawings of Shel Silverstein (1974)

The Giving Tree (1964)

Uncle Shelby's A Giraffe and a Half (1964)

Who Wants a Cheap Rhinoceros? (1964)

Uncle Shelby's Story of Lafcadio, the Lion Who Shot Back (1963)

Silverstein's first children's book, *Uncle Shelby's Story of Lafcadio, the Lion Who Shot Back*, was published in 1963. This book was very popular and sold many copies. But it was Silverstein's next children's book, *The Giving Tree,* that brought him great fame as a children's author.

Silverstein published several more books. He published *Where the Sidewalk Ends: The*

"I would hope that people, no matter what age, would find something to identify with in my books, pick one up and experience a personal sense of discovery. That's great. But for them, not for me."

Poems & Drawings of Shel Silverstein in 1974 and *A Light in the Attic* in 1981. He then took a break from writing children's books for several years and spent most of his time writing plays for adults. He also worked on a screenplay for a movie. Silverstein published his last children's book, *Falling Up: Poems and Drawings,* in 1996.

During his career, Shel Silverstein wrote nine books for children. His books have sold more than 18 million copies and have been translated into twenty languages. Silverstein died on May 8, 1999.

WHERE TO FIND OUT MORE ABOUT SHEL SILVERSTEIN

BOOKS

Meister, Cari. *Shel Silverstein.* Minneapolis: Abdo & Daughters, 2001.

Something about the Author. Vol. 92. Detroit: Gale Research, 1997.

Ward, S. *Meet Shel Silverstein.* New York: PowerKids Press, 2001.

WEB SITES

SHEL SILVERSTEIN ARCHIVE
http://members.tripod.com/~ShelSilverstein/
To find the collected works of Shel Silverstein

SHEL SILVERSTEIN HOME PAGE
http://www.shelsilverstein.com/indexSite.html
For information about the author and his works

TEACHER RESOURCE FILE
http://falcon.jmu.edu/~ramseyil/silverstein.htm
To read a biography of Shel Silverstein

SILVERSTEIN RECORDED HIS OWN COUNTRY MUSIC ALBUM, *THE GREAT CONCH TRAIN ROBBERY,* IN 1980.

Seymour Simon

Born: August 9, 1931

Look closely and listen carefully. Feel the world around you. Wonder about everything you see, hear, and feel. That's the message in the more than 200 science books Seymour Simon has written for middle-grade and high-school readers. Simon is primarily a nonfiction writer, but his fiction books are popular, too.

Seymour Simon was born on August 9, 1931, in New York City. His parents were David Simon and Clara Liftin Simon. As a child, Seymour was fascinated with the how and why of things and showed great interest in science.

Seymour attended the Bronx High School of Science in New York and was president of the Junior Astronomy Club at the American Museum of Natural History.

FOR HIS PROJECTS AND INVESTIGATIONS, SIMON HAS KEPT ROCK COLLECTIONS, WATER SAMPLES, FISH, EARTHWORMS, AND VARIOUS ANIMALS IN HIS HOME. THE COLLECTION LOOKS LIKE A GIANT LABORATORY.

He continued his education in animal studies at City College of New York. Following graduation, he became a teacher.

For more than twenty years, Seymour Simon taught science and creative writing to intermediate and junior high school students in New York City. He used the writing and activities that he developed for his students in the classroom to launch his career in writing.

In 1968, he published his first book, *Animals in Field and Laboratory: Science Projects in Animal Behavior.* Since then, he has published many popular series.

His Discovering series provides guides to the study and care of animals. The On

A Selected Bibliography of Simon's Work

Lungs (2007)
Emergency Vehicles (2006)
Big Bugs (2005)
Cool Cars (2003)
Baby Animals (2002)
Seymour Simon's Book of Trains (2002)
Destination: Mars (2000)
Gorillas (2000)
Crocodiles and Alligators (1999)
The Invisible Man and Other Cases (1998)
Lightning (1997)
Star Walk (1995)
Wolves (1993)
Snakes (1992)
Earthquakes (1991)
Neptune (1991)
Whales (1989)
How to Be an Ocean Scientist in Your Own Home (1988)
Mars (1987)
Uranus (1987)
Chip Rogers, Computer Whiz (1984)
The Dinosaur Is the Biggest Animal That Ever Lived and Other Wrong Ideas You Thought Were True (1984)
Animals in Field an Laboratory: Science Projects in Animal Behavior (1968)

Your Street series encourages children who live in the city to explore their surroundings. He has written on a wide range of topics—from chemistry in the kitchen to the stars and beyond.

In addition to nonfiction, Simon also writes fiction. *Chip Rogers, Computer Whiz,* is a mystery story that introduces readers to computer concepts and basic programming. A series called Einstein Anderson is about kids using science to solve mysteries.

Whether Simon is writing fiction or nonfiction, research is important to him. He tries out each experiment before putting it in a book.

> *"To me, science is a way of finding out about the world. It's easy enough to read what an authority says about a particular subject, but it's so much more satisfying and rewarding to find out the answer to a question by working at it yourself."*

Every investigation begins with a series of questions. Sometimes he provides the answers to the questions he asks. More often, he suggests activities and experiments for readers, so they will come up with the answers on their own.

Simon and his wife, Joyce, live in Great Neck, New York. They have two sons. Although Simon is now a full-time author, he still considers himself a teacher.

SIMON OFTEN WORKS ON SEVERAL BOOKS AT THE SAME TIME. HE CAN BE WRITING ONE BOOK, RESEARCHING ANOTHER, CONTACTING SOURCES FOR INFORMATION ABOUT A THIRD, AND OUTLINING A FOURTH, ALL AT ONCE.

He often visits classrooms and libraries to discuss his books and to hear children's ideas. For him, two of the most important things about being a science teacher and a writer are encouraging discovery and making science fun!

❧

WHERE TO FIND OUT MORE ABOUT SEYMOUR SIMON

BOOKS

McElmeel, Sharron L. *100 Most Popular Children's Authors: Biographical Sketches and Bibliographies.* Englewood, Colo.: Libraries Unlimited, 1999.

Simon, Seymour. *From Paper Airplanes to Outer Space.*
Katonah, N.Y.: Richard C. Owen, 2000.

Something about the Author.
Vol. 73. Detroit: Gale Research, 1993.

WEB SITES

HOUGHTON MIFFLIN MEET THE AUTHOR
http://www.eduplace.com/kids/hmr/mtai/simon.html
To read a biography of Seymour Simon

INTERNET PUBLIC LIBRARY
http://www.ipl.org/kidspace/askauthor/simon.html
To read about Simon's life

SEYMOUR SIMON HOME PAGE
http://www.seymoursimon.com/
To read about Seymour Simon's work, and to find a list of related links

---

SIMON USES A SPECIAL TECHNIQUE TO GET READERS INVOLVED IN HIS BOOKS. HE BEGINS EACH CHAPTER WITH A CAPTIVATING STORY.

Marc Simont

Born: November 23, 1915

Marc Simont has illustrated more than one hundred children's books. His illustrations show a great variety of styles, depending on their subject matter. Sometimes they are humorous and cartoon-like, and other times they are soft, warm, and full of feeling. Whatever his

style, Simont tells a story much better than words alone can do.

Marc Simont was born in 1915 in Paris, France. His parents were originally from the Catalan region of northern Spain. As he was growing up, Marc learned to speak French, English, Spanish, and Catalan.

Marc's father and two of his uncles were artists. His father worked as an illustrator for the French magazine *L'Illustration*, and he encouraged his son's artistic talents from an

---

DURING WORLD WAR II (1939–1945), SIMONT USED HIS ART SKILLS TO PRODUCE VISUAL MATERIALS FOR THE U.S. ARMY.

early age. When Marc was a little boy, his father moved to the United States. Marc then went to live with his uncle in Barcelona, Spain. That's where he began school. Continuing to grow as an artist, he enjoyed sketching the city's bullfighters.

Marc did not complete high school. In his late teens, however, he studied art at the Académie Ranson and Académie Julien in Paris. He also studied with Parisian artist André Lhote. Nevertheless, he always considered his father to be his most influential art teacher.

In 1935, Simont settled in New York City, where he studied for two years at the National Academy of Design. After that, he worked at a

A Selected Bibliography of Simont's Work

The Stray Dog (2001)
The Goose That Almost Got Cooked (1997)
What Happened to the Dinosaurs? (Illustrations only, 1989)
The Dallas Titans Get Ready for Bed (Illustrations only, 1986)
The Year of the Boar and Jackie Robinson (Illustrations only, 1984)
The Philharmonic Gets Dressed (Illustrations only, 1982)
Ten Copycats in a Boat, and Other Riddles (Illustrations only, 1979)
A Space Story (Illustrations only, 1978)
The Star in the Pail (Illustrations only, 1975)
Nate the Great (Illustrations only, 1972)
Afternoon in Spain (1965)
The Trail-Driving Rooster (Illustrations only, 1955)
A Tree Is Nice (Illustrations only, 1955)
The Thirteen Clocks (Illustrations only, 1951)
The Happy Day (Illustrations only, 1949)
The Castle in the Silver Woods (Illustrations only, 1939)
The Pirate of Chatham Square (Illustrations only, 1939)

Simont's Major Literary Awards

2002 Caldecott Honor Book
2001 Boston Globe–Horn Book Picture Book Honor Book
   The Stray Dog
1957 Caldecott Medal
   A Tree Is Nice
1950 Caldecott Honor Book
   The Happy Day

> *"I believe that if I like the drawings I do, children will like them also."*

number of art-related jobs. He painted portraits and murals, made sculptures, and produced advertising illustrations for magazines. He also ventured into children's book illustration, and his first illustrated books came out in 1939. They were *The Pirate of Chatham Square* by Emma G. Sterne and *The Castle in the Silver Woods* by Ruth Bryan Owens.

Simont served in the U.S. Army for three years during World War II (1939–1945). In 1945, he married Sara Dalton, a teacher of handicapped children, and they later had a son who was also named Marc. Meanwhile, Simont went on to illustrate many books for children.

Simont has collaborated with such popular authors as Margaret Wise Brown and James Thurber. Among his best-loved books are *The Happy Day* by Ruth Krause and *A Tree Is Nice* by Janice May Udry. In *The Happy Day*, forest animals wake up to a spring day after a long winter's sleep. *A Tree Is Nice* celebrates the many activities that trees allow us to enjoy—climbing, swinging on branches, raking leaves, and picnicking in their shade.

> *"In the best scenarios, the illustrator will love the story, adopt it as his own, and with his pictures give an added dimension to the book."*

SIMONT ENJOYS MANY SPORTS, INCLUDING SKIING AND SOCCER.

Simont also illustrates the ongoing Nate the Great series by Marjorie Weinman Sharmat. These books are about a boy who does detective work to solve mysteries in his neighborhood.

Besides illustrating others' work, Simont has created the pictures for several books he wrote himself. One is *The Stray Dog*. It's based on the true story of a family who found a scruffy little dog during their picnic. As always, Simont's illustrations lend the story an endearing charm and warmth.

Simont currently lives in West Cornwall, Connecticut.

☙

WHERE TO FIND OUT MORE ABOUT MARC SIMONT

BOOKS

Rockman, Connie C., ed. *Ninth Book of Junior Authors and Illustrators*. New York: H. W. Wilson Company, 2004.

Silvey, Anita, ed. *The Essential Guide to Children's Books and Their Creators*. Boston: Houghton Mifflin Company, 2002.

WEB SITES

CBC MAGAZINE
http://www.cbcbooks.org/cbcmagazine/meet/marc_simont.html
For a biography of the artist

ENCYCLOPAEDIA BRITANNICA
http://www.britannica.com/ebi/article-9336580
To read a biography of the artist

SIMONT BECAME A CITIZEN OF THE UNITED STATES IN 1936.

Peter Sís

Born: May 11, 1949

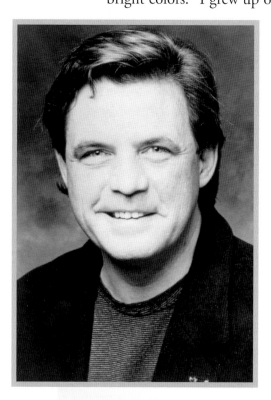

Peter Sís grew up in the former Czechoslovakia in central Europe. When he looked around his hometown, Peter did not see many bright colors. "I grew up on a block of gray houses, with sad people, all with ashen faces, and red flags supplying the only color," Sís notes. When he became an illustrator and artist, Sís decided to use many bright colors in his pictures. He has gone on to write and illustrate nearly twenty books for children. His best-known books include *A Small Tall Tale from the Far Far North, The Three Golden Keys,* and *Komodo!* He also works as a filmmaker and illustrates books written by other children's book authors.

Peter Sís was born on May 11, 1949, in Brno, Czechoslovakia (now the Czech

SÍS RECENTLY CREATED A MURAL FOR THE BALTIMORE-WASHINGTON INTERNATIONAL AIRPORT, A POSTER FOR THE NEW YORK CITY SUBWAY SYSTEM, AND A STAGE SET FOR THE JOFFREY BALLET.

Republic). Growing up in Czechoslovakia was not easy. Peter's family did not have many things. The government did not let people have many freedoms. Food and other supplies were difficult to find.

When Peter was a young boy, his mother encouraged him to draw. He spent much of his time drawing pictures. His father used to tell him stories about his adventures that made Peter want to explore the world. Peter believed that becoming an artist and filmmaker would allow him to make his own adventures.

"The picture book, or the animated film based on the book, can be real art and can influence young people all around the world. With my illustrations I am participating in the future in a world that is in desperate need of feelings, consideration, love, and education."

When he was older, Sís studied painting and filmmaking. He attended art schools in Czechoslovakia and in London, England. Sís became a good filmmaker and won an award in 1980 for a film.

In 1982, the government of Czechoslovakia asked Sís to produce a film. He was sent to Los Angeles, California, to produce a film for the 1984 Winter Olympics. The film project was canceled when Czechoslovakia decided not to compete in the Olympics. Even though Sís was ordered to return to Czechoslovakia, he decided to stay in the United States.

———

SÍS STARTED HIS CAREER PAINTING WITH OIL PAINTS. WHEN HIS DAUGHTER WAS BORN, HE SWITCHED TO WATERCOLOR PAINTS BECAUSE OF THE STRONG FUMES FROM THE OILS.

A Selected Bibliography of Sís's Work

Sís's Major Literary Awards

Sís wanted to find work as an illustrator of children's books. He moved to New York City in 1984 and was hired by many publishing companies to illustrate children's books. Books that included Sís's illustrations won many awards. The first book he wrote and illustrated, *Rainbow Rhino,* was published in 1987.

Peter Sís became a U.S. citizen in 1988. He is a talented artist aside from his work on children's books. He has created more than 1,000 illustrations for

"I see things much like a ten-year-old child, like people waving for taxis and riding in elevators. I did not see this in Prague. So I write about them."

magazines and newspapers. His artwork has been displayed in galleries and museums throughout the world.

Peter Sís continues to write and illustrate children's books. He is frequently asked to create artwork for many other purposes, including posters and book jackets. He lives in New York City with his family.

❧

WHERE TO FIND OUT MORE ABOUT PETER SÍS

BOOKS
Cummings, Pat, ed. *Talking with Artists, Vol. 3, Conversations with Peter Catalanotto, Raul Colon, Lisa Desimini, Jane Dyer, Kevin Hawkes, G. Brian Karas, Betsy Lewin, Ted Lewin, Keiko Narahashi, Elise Primavera, Anna Rich, Peter Sís and Paul O. Zelinsky.* Boston: Houghton Mifflin, 1999.

Kovacs, Deborah, and James Preller. *Meet the Authors and Illustrators: 60 Creators of Favorite Children's Books Talk about Their Work.* Vol. 2. New York: Scholastic, 1993.

WEB SITES
EMBRACING THE CHILD
http://embracingthechild.org/Bookspecialsis_.htm
To read short descriptions of Peter Sís's books

HORN BOOK STUDIO VIEWS
http://www.hbook.com/publications/magazine/articles/mar98_sis.asp
To read an excerpt from an interview with Peter Sís

TIBET THROUGH THE RED BOX
http://www.petersistibet.com/
To read about the book *Tibet: Through the Red Box* and its author, Peter Sís

---

WATERCOLOR PAINTINGS CAN TAKE A LONG TIME TO DRY. SÍS OFTEN PUTS HIS PAINTINGS NEAR THE OVEN TO DRY WHILE HE COOKS DINNER FOR HIS FAMILY.

William Sleator

Born: February 13, 1945

Whoever ventures into one of William Sleator's books is in for a wild ride. His stories for children and young adults are filled with hair-raising, suspense-filled adventures.

William Warner Sleator III was born in 1945 in Havre de Grace, Maryland. With his sister and two brothers, he grew up in University City, Missouri, a suburb of Saint Louis. William began studying piano when he was six, and he started writing stories at about the same time. He loved writing spooky tales, and one of his first stories was called "The Haunted Easter Egg." Comic books and science fiction stories were his favorite reading materials—especially if they were frightful. "I was fascinated by the grotesque and the macabre," he recalls.

In high school, William kept up his music studies as well as his writing. He even wrote a musical composition that his school orchestra performed. After graduation, he attended Harvard University in Cambridge, Massachusetts. He began as a music major

---

SLEATOR'S BOOK *ODDBALLS* IS A COLLECTION OF STORIES LOOSELY BASED ON HIS OWN CHILDHOOD AND ADOLESCENCE.

but switched to English, earning a degree in 1967.

Sleator then took off for London, England, where he studied musical composition. To earn a living, he worked as a pianist accompanying ballet dancers in the Royal Ballet School and the Rambert School. It was during this time that he wrote his first

> *"I . . . use real people in my books, and that has gotten me into trouble at times."*

children's book, *The Angry Moon*. Published in 1970, it's the retelling of a Native American legend.

In England, Sleator lived in an old cottage in the midst of a forest with his elderly landlady. The cottage had once been a "pest house" where people with smallpox were isolated from the rest of the population. This setting gave him the idea for his first young-adult book, *Blackbriar*. It recounts the spooky adventures of a teenage boy who lives in a haunted cottage in the countryside.

Sleator returned to the United States and settled in Boston, Massachusetts. There he worked as a pianist for the Boston Ballet Company from 1974 to 1983. He toured the United States and Europe with the dance company and even wrote the music for three of its ballets.

A COMMON THEME IN SLEATOR'S BOOKS IS SIBLING RIVALRY, OR CONFLICT AMONG BROTHERS AND SISTERS.

A Selected Bibliography of Sleator's Work

The Last Universe (2005)
The Boy Who Couldn't Die (2004)
Marco's Millions (2001)
The Beasties (1997)
Dangerous Wishes (1995)
Oddballs (1993)
The Spirit House (1991)
The Boy Who Reversed Himself (1986)
Singularity (1985)
Interstellar Pig (1984)
Fingers (1983)
The Green Futures of Tycho (1981)
Into the Dream (1979)
House of Stairs (1974)
Blackbriar (1972)
The Angry Moon (1970)

Sleator's Major Literary Awards

1971 Caldecott Honor Book
1971 Boston Globe–Horn Book Picture Book Honor Book
   The Angry Moon

Meanwhile, Sleator continued writing books for young people. Most of his works are fantasy, mystery, or science fiction stories with chilling plots. In *House of Stairs*, for example, five teenagers are stuck inside a cruel scientific experiment that rewards hostile behavior. In *Interstellar Pig*, a teenager's next-door neighbors turn out to be evil space aliens whom he must battle for his life.

> *"A lot of the fun of writing science fiction is learning about real scientific phenomena, like behavior modification or black holes or the fourth dimension, and turning them into stories."*

The Spirit House and its sequel, *Dangerous Wishes*, revolve around spiritual beliefs in Thailand. For these books, Sleator was close to his subject. He built a farmhouse in northeastern Thailand, and he now spends half the year there. He enjoys writing, as he says, "with a beautiful view of checkerboard rice fields, brilliantly green in the rainy season." For the other half of the year, he lives in Boston.

❧

WHERE TO FIND OUT MORE ABOUT WILLIAM SLEATOR

BOOKS

Kovacs, Deborah, ed. *Meet the Authors and Illustrators: Sixty Creators of Favorite Children's Books Talk about Their Work.* New York: Scholastic, 1993.

Pendergast, Tom, and Sara Pendergast, eds. *St. James Guide to Young Adult Writers.* 2nd ed. Detroit: St. James, 1999.

Silvey, Anita, ed. *The Essential Guide to Children's Books and Their Creators.* Boston: Houghton Mifflin Company, 2002.

WEB SITES
PENGUIN GROUP
http://us.penguingroup.com/nf/Author/AuthorPage/0,,0_1000030218,00.html
For information on why William Sleator wanted to become an author

TYCHO
http://www.tycho.org/
For information about *The Green Futures of Tycho*

WILLIAM SLEATOR HOME PAGE
www.cscmu.edu/~sleator/billy
For contact information

———

SLEATOR DEDICATED *THE GREEN FUTURES OF TYCHO* TO HIS BROTHER TYCHO.

David Small

Born: February 12, 1945

For many years, David Small was happy to teach others what he knew about art and drawing. But when he was laid off from his teaching job, he needed to think fast. What could he do? With the encouragement of his wife, Small tried his hand at writing and illustrating books for children.

Since his first book was published in 1982, David Small has created nearly thirty books for kids. He has earned fans far and wide for his fun stories and bright, colorful pictures.

David Small was born on February 12, 1945, in Detroit, Michigan. As a boy, he was very sick. David spent a lot of time in bed trying to get better. During that time, he often read books or drew pictures. David's mother recognized his special talent and signed him up for Saturday art classes at the Detroit Institute of Arts. Although David hated the

AS A BOY, DAVID SMALL SPENT MANY SUMMERS ON HIS GRANDPARENTS' FARM IN INDIANA. THERE, HE LEARNED TO LOVE ANIMALS AND THE COUNTRY.

classes, he loved looking through the museum. He enjoyed roaming the big building, examining the pictures, armor, and other items.

When Small entered Wayne State Univeristy, his interest in art really blossomed. He spent as much time as he could working on his art. He knew he wanted to focus on art and drawing when he graduated. After earning a master of fine arts degree from Yale University in 1972, Small began teaching art to college students. In time, he turned to illustrating—and writing—children's books.

"Though I always dreamed of being an artist, it was not until I was in my late thirties and had several works published that I began to say, proudly, 'I am an artist.' I took it that seriously."

Small's stories usually carry a positive message. Many of his books focus on independent characters who are different from others. One of Small's most popular books is *Imogene's Antlers.* The story about a girl who sprouts antlers overnight is a favorite of kids everywhere. The book has sold more than a million copies and been translated into many different languages.

It usually takes Small about a year to create a book from start to finish. Although he prefers writing and illustrating his own ideas, Small also enjoys drawing pictures for the stories of other authors. Over the years, he has brought to life the works of several famous writers. They include Carl

SOME OF SMALL'S BOOK ILLUSTRATIONS HANG ON THE WALL OF HIS OFFICE. HE CALLS THE PICTURES HIS "FAMILY PORTRAITS."

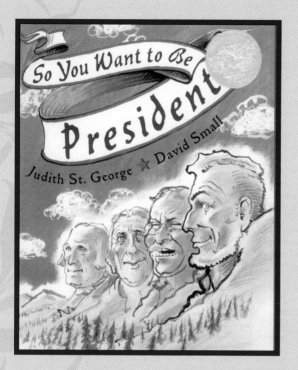

A Selected Bibliography of Small's Work

Once Upon a Banana (Illustrations only, 2006)

When Dinosaurs Came with Everything (Illustrations only, 2006)

Friend (Illustrations only, 2004)

Essential Worldwide Monster Guide (Illustrations only, 2003)

So You Want to Be an Inventor? (2002)

The Journey (Illustrations only, 2001)

So You Want to Be President? (Illustrations only, 2000)

The Library (Illustrations only, 1999)

The Gardener (Illustrations only, 1997)

Hoover's Bride (1995)

George Washington's Cows (1994)

The Money Tree (Illustrations only, 1994)

Box and Cox (Illustrations only, 1990)

As: A Surfeit of Similes (Illustrations only, 1989)

Imogene's Antlers (1985)

Eulalie and the Hopping Head (1982)

Small's Major Literary Awards

2001 Caldecott Medal
  So You Want to Be President?

1998 Caldecott Honor Book
  The Gardener

Sandburg, Jonathan Swift, Beverly Cleary, Russell Hoban, and Norton Juster. He also worked with author Judith St. George on *So You Want to Be President?*—which won the Caldecott Medal in 2001.

One of Small's favorite writers to work with is Sarah Stewart. Stewart is not only a talented children's author—she's Small's wife! Together, the couple has created several popular books for children, including *The Library, The Gardener,* and *The Journey. The Gardener* was named a Caldecott Honor Book.

Small and Stewart live in a big, old house in Mendon, Michigan. Small has livened up their home by painting pictures of insects, plants, and other things all over the walls.

In addition to children's books, David Small draws editorial cartoons for such papers as the *New York Times,* the *Wall Street Journal,* and the *Washington Post.* His pictures also appear in national magazines. Fans of Small's children's books can rest assured that they'll see more of his illustrations in the future. This talented artist believes that his best work is yet to come.

"I'm a perfectionist, but it's good to set high standards for yourself."

❧

WHERE TO FIND OUT MORE ABOUT DAVID SMALL

BOOKS

Holtze, Sally Holmes, ed.
Sixth Book of Junior Authors & Illustrators.
New York: H. W. Wilson Company, 1989.

McElmeel, Sharron L. *100 Most Popular Picture Book Authors and Illustrators: Biographical Sketches and Bibliographies.* Englewood, Colo.: Libraries Unlimited, 2000.

Silvey, Anita, ed. *The Essential Guide to Children's Books and Their Creators.* Boston: Houghton Mifflin Company, 2002.

WEB SITES

NATIONAL CENTER FOR CHILDREN'S
ILLUSTRATED LITERATURE
http://www.nccil.org/small.html
For a biography of David Small

PARENTS' CHOICE
http://www.parents-choice.org/full_abstract.cfm?art_id=22&the_page=editorials
To learn more about Small's life

———

SMALL'S FIRST BOOK, PUBLISHED IN **1982,** WAS *EULALIE AND THE HOPPING HEAD.* SMALL SENT THE BOOK TO MORE THAN TWENTY PUBLISHERS BEFORE IT WAS FINALLY ACCEPTED.

Lane Smith

Born: August 25, 1959

Lane Smith is known for his wild illustrations in books such as *The Stinky Cheese Man and Other Fairly Stupid Tales* and *Squids Will Be Squids: Fresh Morals, Beastly Fables.* His characters are grotesque, with huge heads and tiny bodies, and he likes to use colors such as glow-in-the-dark green and storm-cloud gray.

Some people find his pictures dark and disturbing. "When I was a child, I *liked* dark things," Smith explains. He loved monster movies and Halloween and the scratching of branches against the windows on rainy nights.

Smith was born on August 25, 1959, in Oklahoma, but he grew up in California with his parents and his brother Shane. ("Shane and Lane. My mom thought that was funny," Smith says. "Yeah, a real hoot.") Smith attended California Art Center College of Design in Pasadena.

LANE SMITH WAS CHOSEN TO DO NEW ILLUSTRATIONS FOR ONE OF THE BOOKS DR. SEUSS LEFT UNFINISHED AT THE TIME OF HIS DEATH. *HOORAY FOR DIFFENDOOFER DAY!* ALSO CONTAINED NEW MATERIAL WRITTEN BY JACK PRELUTSKY.

He studied advertising art, but he became interested in pop art and European illustration. His teachers told him he would never find a job.

Smith was lucky, though. He moved to New York and discovered that many magazine editors wanted "punk" and "new wave" illustration—just the kind of thing that he liked to draw. He was soon working for magazines such as *Rolling Stone, Ms.,* and *Time.*

His first children's book was a Halloween-themed alphabet book. Lane painted pictures for all the letters of the alphabet. Then an author named Eve Merriam took the pictures and wrote poems to fit them. *Halloween ABC* was published in 1987.

A Selected Bibliography of Smith's Work

John, Paul, George & Ben (2006)
Happy Hocky Family Moves to the Country! (2004)
Pinocchio, the Boy: Incognito in Collodi (2002)
Baloney, Henry P. (Illustrations only, 2001)
The Very Persistent Gappers of Frip (Illustrations only, 2000)
It's All Greek to Me (Illustrations only, 1999)
Hooray for Diffendoofer Day! (Illustrations only, 1998)
Squids Will Be Squids: Fresh Morals, Beastly Fables (1998)
James and the Giant Peach (Illustrations only, 1996)
Tut, Tut (Illustrations only, 1996)
Math Curse (Illustrations only, 1995)
The Happy Hocky Family (1993)
The Stinky Cheese Man and Other Fairly Stupid Tales (Illustrations only, 1992)
The Big Pets (1991)
Glasses: Who Needs 'Em? (1991)
Time Warp Trio: Knights of the Kitchen Table (Illustrations only, 1991)
Time Warp Trio: The Not-So-Jolly Roger (Illustrations only, 1991)
Flying Jake (1989)
The True Story of the 3 Little Pigs! (Illustrations only, 1989)
Halloween ABC (Illustrations only, 1987)

Smith's Major Literary Awards

1993 Caldecott Honor Book
   The Stinky Cheese Man and Other Fairly Stupid Tales

Smith has created several books on his own, including *Flying Jake* and *Glasses: Who Needs 'Em?* But his best-known work has been with Jon Scieszka, a teacher and aspiring writer he met in the 1980s. Scieszka's sense of humor fits well with Smith's drawing style. The first book the two did together was *The True Story of the 3 Little Pigs!* It was published in 1989, and in it, the wolf, the villain of the tale, explains why he is innocent. It took a long time to find a publisher for the strange book. But once the book was published, it became wildly popular—even the writer and artist were surprised.

Smith and Scieszka were invited to speak at schools. They started telling other twisted-around versions of fairy tales to entertain the children they met. These tales became *The Stinky Cheese Man and Other Fairly Stupid Tales,* another very popular book. In *The Stinky Cheese Man,* the ugly duckling grows up to be an ugly duck, and a princess kisses a frog only to discover that he's just kidding about being a prince. The book has many jokes about bookmaking, too. The title page is in the wrong spot, the dedication is upside-down, and several characters are crushed when the table of contents falls onto the page.

"I just love the print medium. I always thought it would be kind of depressing to work for months on a painting and then . . . have it hang in somebody's house."

TO EARN MONEY FOR COLLEGE, SMITH WORKED AS A JANITOR AT DISNEYLAND. HE SPENT THE NIGHTS CLEANING OUT THE HAUNTED MANSION AND RIDES SUCH AS THE REVOLVING TEACUPS.

> *"Most of the magazine work I do, they'll call Monday and need it finished by Wednesday. If I really buckle down, I can probably do a painting a day, but I like to take a lot of breaks."*

Scieszka and Smith have created several other picture books together. They also started the Time Warp Trio series, about three boys who travel through time and have goofy adventures.

A reporter once asked Lane Smith whether he planned to keep on doing silly work. "There are so many serious books out there and lots of people who do them really well," Smith told him. "But there aren't many people who do really goofy work."

WHERE TO FIND OUT MORE ABOUT LANE SMITH

BOOKS

Kovacs, Deborah, and James Preller. *Meet the Authors and Illustrators: 60 Creators of Favorite Children's Books Talk about Their Work.* Vol. 2. New York: Scholastic, 1993.

Silvey, Anita, ed. *The Essential Guide to Children's Books and Their Creators.* Boston: Houghton Mifflin Company, 2002.

WEB SITES

BALONEY, HENRY P.
http://www.baloneyhenryp.com/
For information about Jon Scieszka and Lane Smith and special information about the book *Baloney, Henry P.*

LANE'S FIRST MEETING WITH SCIESZKA WASN'T VERY SUCCESSFUL. THE TWO WENT TO THE BRONX ZOO IN NEW YORK. SMITH WANTED TO TALK, BUT SCIESZKA JUST TOLD KNOCK-KNOCK JOKES. "I THOUGHT, WHAT'S WITH THIS GUY?" SMITH REMEMBERS.

Lemony Snicket

Born: 1970

Lemony Snicket didn't like many of the books that he read as a child. He thought they were too happy, and he didn't like happy endings—or happy beginnings or happy middles. And so the unlikely children's author wrote about all the things that parents want to shield their children from. He wrote about the disasters that descend on the unluckiest of children. He wrote about parents killed by fire, orphans hated by their relatives, and children forever on the run from a cruel villain. He wrote, in short, A Series of Unfortunate Events, and along the way, he made legions of children very happy.

Lemony Snicket likes to say that his own childhood was

DANIEL HANDLER FIRST USED THE NAME LEMONY SNICKET WHEN HE WAS RESEARCHING A BOOK. HE DIDN'T WANT THE PEOPLE HE WAS WRITING ABOUT TO KNOW WHO HE WAS.

unspeakably dreadful, but Lemony Snicket is, in fact, not a real person at all. He is the creation of Daniel Handler, whose own childhood seems not to have been so bad. He was born in 1970 in San Francisco, California. Unlike the unfortunate children in his books, his parents were not killed by fire. One is an accountant, and one a college dean. Handler went to school at San Francisco's Lowell High School,

> *"There are species of insects which spend their entire lives in filthy underground caverns. Compared to those species of insects—and certain others—my childhood was 'happy' indeed."*
> —Lemony Snicket

received a good education, and graduated with an award for the best personality. That doesn't sound so bad. Handler then went to Wesleyan University in Middletown, Connecticut. He started to write poetry and in 1990 won a prize from the Academy of American Poets. His love of poets can be seen in the names of the characters in his books: the Baudelaire children are named after a famous French poet. There is also a Mr. Poe, named for Edgar Allan Poe, the American poet who himself wrote rather morbid tales.

After graduating from college, Handler received an Olin Fellowship to write a novel. He also worked as a comedy writer for a radio

THE AUDIO VERSION OF LEMONY SNICKET'S *THE BAD BEGINNING* WAS NOMINATED FOR A GRAMMY AWARD FOR THE BEST SPOKEN WORD ALBUM FOR CHILDREN.

THE BAD BEGINNING

A Selected Bibliography of Snicket's Work

The End (2006)
The Beatrice Letters (2006)
The Penultimate Peril (2005)
The Ominous Omnibus (2005)
Behind the Scenes with Count Olaf (2004)
The Grim Grotto (2004)
The Slippery Slope (2003)
The Carnivorous Carnival (2002)
Lemony Snicket: the Unauthorized Autobiography. (2002)
The Ersatz Elevator (2001)
The Hostile Hospital (2001)
The Vile Village (2001)
The Austere Academy (2000)
The Miserable Mill (2000)
The Wide Window (2000)
The Bad Beginning (1999)
The Reptile Room (1999)

program called "The House of Blues Radio Hour." It might seem odd that the morbid Mr. Handler was a comedy writer, but beneath his dreary statements is a wry smile. His two adult novels both deal with the dark humor of bad situations. When an editor suggested he turn his wicked humor into children's books, his book series called A Series of Unfortunate Events was the outcome.

Under the name Lemony Snicket, Handler writes about the misadventures of the three Baudelaire children: Violet, Klaus, and Sunny. The children are clever and speak in a deadpan manner. Handler believes that kids are smart, and his writing is complicated and witty. Snicket himself often butts into the story to make a few remarks about the writing style and to warn readers of especially dreadful things to come.

> *"Don't read my books!"*
> —*Lemony Snicket*

Lemony Snicket also warns his readers not to read his books. But no one is listening—his books are frequently on best-seller lists. They have delighted children who find dreadful things funny and who like the strange Lemony Snicket, even if Daniel Handler sometimes pretends that he doesn't exist.

❧

WHERE TO FIND OUT MORE ABOUT LEMONY SNICKET

BOOKS

Snicket, Lemony. *Lemony Snicket: The Unauthorized Autobiography.* New York: HarperCollins, 2002.

Rockman, Connie C., ed. *The Ninth Book of Junior Authors and Illustrators.* New York: H. W. Wilson Company, 2004.

WEB SITES

DYMOCKS BOOKSELLERS
http://www.dymocks.com.au/contentstatic/literarymatter/interviews/lemonysnicket.asp
For the transcript of an interview with Snicket

LEMONY SNICKET HOME PAGE
www.lemonysnicket.com/
For as much autobiographical information as Lemony Snicket is willing to offer, a booklist, and some frequently asked questions

---

WHEN HANDLER SHOWS UP AT BOOK READINGS, HE EXPLAINS THAT HE IS STANDING IN FOR LEMONY SNICKET. HE LIKES TO MAKE UP FOR SNICKET'S ABSENCE BY PLAYING THE ACCORDION.

Zilpha Keatley Snyder

Born: May 11, 1927

Mystery and magic, witches and ghosts—these are some of the themes young readers can expect from Zilpha Keatley Snyder. Among the dozens of books she has authored, many are based on her own childhood fantasies.

Zilpha Keatley was born in Lemoore, California, in 1927. The Keatleys lived in a rural area, and they kept lots of animals. Zilpha loved playing with the family's dogs, cats, horses, chickens, rabbits,

goats, and cows. She loved reading, too. Soon after she learned to read at age four, she began making regular trips to the library. Through reading, she found she could escape into wonderful, imaginary worlds.

Zilpha's father had been a rancher for years, and her mother was a schoolteacher. Both parents told her fascinating stories about the

IN 1985, SNYDER FULFILLED A LIFELONG DREAM BY TAKING A TRIP TO EGYPT.

past. Zilpha herself began writing stories as a girl. At age eight, she decided she would be a professional writer someday.

Zilpha had skipped a grade in elementary school, so she was a year younger than her classmates. This made her shy, and she withdrew even more into reading. For a whole year, she read whatever she could find about ancient Egypt.

After high school, she enrolled in Whittier College in Whittier, California. There she met a music major named Larry Allan Snyder, whom she married in 1950. After graduation in 1948, she taught elementary school at Washington School in Berkeley, California. She

"I enjoy writing for an audience that shares my optimism, curiosity, and freewheeling imagination."

and Larry later had two children—Susan and Douglas.

The Snyders moved around the country as Larry attended graduate schools and served in the U.S. Air Force. Zilpha taught in New York, Washington, and Alaska. In 1958, the family moved to Berkeley, where Zilpha became a master teacher and demonstrator for education classes at the University of California.

Once the family was settled in Berkeley, Snyder began to think again about becoming a writer. She remembered a dream she had had

---

SNYDER'S BOOK *BELOW THE ROOT* WAS MADE INTO A COMPUTER GAME IN **1984.**

A Selected Bibliography of Snyder's Work

The Unseen (2004)
Gib Rides Home (1998)
Libby on Wednesday (1990)
And Condors Danced (1987)
The Changing Maze (1985)
Blair's Nightmare (1984)
The Birds of Summer (1983)
A Fabulous Creature (1981)
Until the Celebration (1977)
And All Between (1976)
Below the Root (1975)
The Witches of Worm (1972)
The Headless Cupid (1971)
The Changeling (1970)
The Egypt Game (1967)
The Velvet Room (1965)
Season of Ponies (1964)

Snyder's Major Literary Awards

1973 Newbery Honor Book
   The Witches of Worm

1972 Newbery Honor Book
   The Headless Cupid

1968 Newbery Honor Book
   The Egypt Game

when she was twelve about some enchanting horses, and she decided to turn it into a children's story. This became her first book, *Season of Ponies*. After two rewrites, it was finally published in 1964. Another early book—*The Egypt Game*—draws on Snyder's childhood fascination with ancient Egypt.

In 1966, the Snyders adopted a little boy from China, whom they named Ben. Four years later, the family took a tour of Europe, returning to settle in an old farmhouse in Santa Rosa, California. Here, Snyder began writing in earnest.

Her stories often have mysterious, magical themes. Several books feature the spooky adventures of the five children in the Stanley family. The three books in Snyder's Green-Sky Trilogy—*Below the Root*, *And All Between*, and *Until the Celebration*— are about people who live in the treetops and deal with the evil beings who dwell underground. For these stories, Snyder drew on a childhood fantasy about creatures that lived beneath the roots of the trees.

Snyder currently lives in Mill Valley, California.

> *"[As a child,] my world might have been quite narrow and uninteresting if it had not been for two magical ingredients— animals and books."*

✣

WHERE TO FIND OUT MORE ABOUT ZILPHA KEATLEY SNYDER

BOOKS

Chevalier, Tracy, ed. *Twentieth Century Children's Writers*. 3rd ed. Detroit: St. Martin's, 1999.

McElmeel, Sharron L. *100 Most Popular Children's Authors: Biographical Sketches and Bibliographies*. Englewood, Colo.: Libraries Unlimited, 1999.

Silvey, Anita, ed. *The Essential Guide to Children's Books and Their Creators*. Boston: Houghton Mifflin Company, 2002.

WEB SITES

RANDOM HOUSE
http://www.randomhouse.com/teachers/authors/results.pperl?authorid=58062
To read about the author

ZILPHA KEATLEY SNYDER HOME PAGE
http://www.zksnyder.com/
For a Web site about the author

———

FOR *GIB RIDES HOME*, SNYDER DREW ON HER FATHER'S CHILDHOOD EXPERIENCES IN AN ORPHANAGE IN NEBRASKA.

Donald Sobol

Born: October 4, 1924

Challenging readers to solve mysteries is what author Donald Sobol does best. In his ever-popular series, Encyclopedia Brown, Sobol invites readers to match wits with ten-year-old detective Leroy Brown. For more than forty years, these detective stories have been entertaining children. They have also helped children learn how to think. Though Donald Sobol is best known for Encyclopedia Brown, he has written historical novels and biographies of famous people as well.

Donald Sobol was born in New York City on October 4, 1924, to Ira J. and Ida Sobol. As a youngster, he dreamed of becoming a singer, a sculptor, and a baseball player, but he soon found these goals quite unreachable. After graduating from the Fieldston School in New York City, Sobol enlisted in the U.S. Army Corp of Engineers

---

TWENTY-SIX PUBLISHERS REJECTED DONALD SOBOL'S FIRST BOOK IN THE ENCYCLOPEDIA BROWN SERIES BEFORE THE T. NELSON PUBLISHING COMPANY FINALLY PUBLISHED IT IN 1963.

and served three years in World War II (1939–1945).

After leaving the army in 1946, he enrolled at Oberlin College in Ohio, where he graduated with a bachelor's degree in English. While Sobol was at Oberlin, an English professor helped him develop his talent for writing.

For the next eight years, Sobol wrote under different names for magazines. Because the pay was low, he had to take

> "Stories originate in two ways. They start from a writer's own experience, or they start from his imagination. Most of my stories depend upon my imagination."

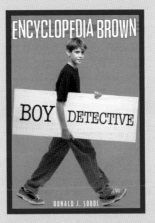

A Selected Bibliography of Sobol's Work

The Two-Minute Mysteries Collection (2004)
Encyclopedia Brown and the Case of the Jumping Frogs (2003)
Encyclopedia Brown and the Case of the Slippery Salamander (1999)
Encyclopedia Brown and the Case of the Sleeping Dog (1998)
Encyclopedia Brown and the Case of the Disgusting Sneakers (1990)
Encyclopedia Brown and the Case of the Treasure Hunt (1988)
Encyclopedia Brown's Book of Wacky Cars (1987)
Encyclopedia Brown's Third Record Book of Weird and Wonderful Facts (1985)
Encyclopedia Brown's Book of Wacky Animals (1985)
Encyclopedia Brown's Book of Wacky Spies (1984)
Encyclopedia Brown Takes the Cake! A Cook and Case Book (1983)
Encyclopedia Brown Sets the Pace (1982)
Angie's First Case (1981)
Encyclopedia Brown Carries On (1980)
Encyclopedia Brown and the Case of the Midnight Visitor (1977)
Encyclopedia Brown and the Case of the Dead Eagles (1976)
Encyclopedia Brown Lends a Hand (1974)
Encyclopedia Brown Takes the Case: Ten All-New Mysteries (1973)
Greta the Strong (1970)
Encyclopedia Brown Keeps the Peace (1969)
Encyclopedia Brown Solves Them All (1968)
Encyclopedia Brown Gets His Man (1967)
Secret Agents Four (1967)
Encyclopedia Brown Finds the Clues (1966)
Encyclopedia Brown and the Case of the Secret Pitch: Ten All-New Mysteries (1965)
Encyclopedia Brown, Boy Detective (1963)
The First Book of Medieval Man (1959)
The Lost Dispatch: A Story of Antietam (1958)
The Double Quest (1957)

extra jobs to support himself. From 1946 to 1952, he worked as a reporter with the *New York Sun* and the *Long Island Daily Press.* Then he worked briefly as a buyer for R. H. Macy in New York City. In 1954, at the age of thirty, Sobol made a daring move. He quit his jobs to write full-time.

"[The advice] 'Write about what you know' had limited me to my own experiences and so forced me to rely solely upon my imagination. 'Know what you write about' set me free. . . . [I] went to the library and dug up all the information I could find."

A year later, he married Rose Tiplitz, an engineer. Together, they had four children. In 1961, they moved to Florida for the winter. They have lived there ever since.

Donald Sobol published his first book in 1957. Called *The Double Quest,* it is a mystery about knights in medieval times. *The Double Quest* and Sobol's next two books—*The Lost Dispatch: A Story of Antietam,* published in 1958, and *The First Book of Medieval Man,* published in 1959—are young-adult books. They were well received but never became as popular as the Encyclopedia Brown books that Sobol began to publish in 1963.

The first title of the series, *Encyclopedia Brown, Boy Detective,* set the pattern for the more than twenty books that followed. Each book contains ten short mysteries on pages filled with jokes. Readers need to

THE ENCYCLOPEDIA BROWN SERIES HAS BEEN TRANSLATED INTO THIRTEEN LANGUAGES AND BRAILLE. SOME OF THEM HAVE BEEN MADE INTO COMIC STRIPS. IN 1989, *ENCYCLOPEDIA BROWN, BOY DETECTIVE* WAS MADE INTO A MOVIE FOR HBO TELEVISION.

do good detective work to discover the clues in the stories and solve the cases without reading the solutions in the back of the book.

Many people compare Donald Sobol's popular Encyclopedia Brown series to the Hardy Boys and Nancy Drew mysteries of the past. For generations, these series have been outwitting readers and making them laugh. Donald Sobol's books will continue to do that for decades to come.

∾

WHERE TO FIND OUT MORE ABOUT DONALD SOBOL

BOOKS

Chevalier, Tracy, ed. *Twentieth-Century Children's Writers.* Chicago: St. James Press, 1989.

De Montreville, Doris, and Elizabeth D. Crawford, eds. *Fourth Book of Junior Authors & Illustrators.* New York: H. W. Wilson Company, 1978.

Silvey, Anita, ed. *The Essential Guide to Children's Books and Their Creators.* Boston: Houghton Mifflin Company, 2002.

WEB SITE

KIDSREAD.COM
http://www.kidsreads.com/series/series-brown-author.asp
For information about Sobol's life and work

———

WHEN ASKED IF ENCYCLOPEDIA BROWN IS A REAL BOY, DONALD SOBOL SAYS, "HE IS, PERHAPS, THE BOY I WANTED TO BE—DOING THE THINGS I WANTED TO READ ABOUT BUT COULD NOT FIND IN ANY BOOK WHEN I WAS TEN."

Gary Soto

Born: April 12, 1952

Growing up in a working-class Mexican American neighborhood has had a strong influence on Gary Soto's writing. His books of poetry and short stories for children and young people include memories of his Mexican American heritage. Some of Soto's best-known books for young people are *Baseball in April and Other Stories, A Fire in My Hands: A Book of Poems, Taking Sides,* and *Neighborhood Odes.*

Soto was born on April 12, 1952, in Fresno, California. Soto's grandparents had come to the United States from Mexico in the 1930s. Soto's parents were born in the United States, but remembered their heritage.

GARY SOTO IS ONE OF THE YOUNGEST POETS TO HAVE HIS WORK PUBLISHED IN *THE NORTON ANTHOLOGY OF MODERN POETRY.*

Gary Soto's parents worked in the fields picking grapes, oranges, and cotton. His father got a job in a factory that packed raisins. When Gary was about five years old, his father died in an accident at the factory. His mother had to raise her three children alone.

Gary's family was poor, and his mother worked hard to provide for her children. Gary did not have books as a child and was not encouraged to read. "I don't think I had any literary aspirations when I was a kid," Soto remembers. "So my wanting to write poetry was sort of a fluke." He did not become interested in writing and poetry until he entered college.

> "One of the things I would like to do is make that leap from being a Chicano writer to being simply a writer."

In 1970, Soto graduated from high school and enrolled at Fresno City College. He planned to study geography, but after taking a poetry class, he became interested in creative writing. Soto loved the poetry that he read for class, and he learned a great deal about poetry from his professors. Soto graduated from college in 1974 and went on to get a master's degree in creative writing.

In 1977, Soto was hired to teach at the University of California at Irvine. He worked as a professor of Chicano studies and English. That same year, he published his first book of poetry for adults, *The Elements of San Joaquin.* In 1985, he won an American Book Award for the

---

SOTO WROTE THE LYRICS FOR THE OPERA *NERDLANDIA*, WHICH WAS PERFORMED BY THE LOS ANGELES OPERA.

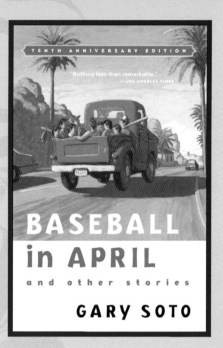

A Selected Bibliography of Soto's Work

Accidental Love (2006)

Help Wanted: Stories (2005)

One Kind of Faith (2003)

If the Shoe Fits (2002)

Poetry Lover (2001)

Nickel and Dime (2000)

A Natural Man (1999)

Big Bushy Mustache (1998)

Buried Onions (1997)

Boys at Work (1995)

Canto Familiar (1995)

Chato's Kitchen (1995)

Summer on Wheels (1995)

Too Many Tamales (1993)

A Fire in My Hands: A Book of Poems (1992)

Neighborhood Odes (1992)

Pacific Crossing (1992)

The Skirt (1992)

Taking Sides (1991)

Baseball in April and Other Stories (1990)

A Summer Life (1990)

Soto's Major Literary Awards

1996 Pura Belpré Honor Book for Narrative
  Baseball in April and Other Stories

memoir *Living up the Street: Narrative Recollections.* Soto did not complete his first book specifically for young people until 1990 when *Baseball in April and Other Stories* was published.

In his stories and poetry, Gary Soto writes about life in his Mexican American neighborhood. He writes about what life was like in large cities and tells stories about the hard work that Mexican Americans did in the fields. In his stories for young people, he writes about realistic situations and conflicts. Most young people can identify with the characters in Soto's books.

In addition to being a writer, Soto has taught creative writing at colleges and universities. He lives in Berkeley,

California, with his
wife and daughter.
He continues to write
poetry, stories, and
plays for young people
and adults.

> *"To me the finest praise is when a reader says, 'I can see your stories.' This is what I'm always working for, a story that becomes alive and meaningful in the reader's mind."*

WHERE TO FIND OUT MORE ABOUT GARY SOTO

BOOKS

Drew, Bernard A. *The 100 Most Popular Young Adult Authors: Biographical Sketches and Bibliographies.* Englewood, Colo.: Libraries Unlimited, 1997.

Hill, Christine M. *Ten Terrific Authors for Teens.* Berkeley Heights, N.J.: Enslow, 2000.

Machamer, Gene. *The Illustrated Hispanic American Profiles.* Mechanicsburg, Pa.: Carlisle Press, 1993.

Soto, Gary. *A Summer Life.* Hanover, N.H.: University Press of New England, 1990.

WEB SITE

GARY SOTO HOME PAGE
http://www.garysoto.com/
For information about Gary Soto's life and work

WHEN GARY SOTO WAS YOUNG, HE WANTED TO BE A PRIEST OR A PALEONTOLOGIST, A SCIENTIST WHO STUDIES FOSSILS AND DINOSAUR BONES.

Elizabeth George Speare

Born: November 21, 1908
Died: November 15, 1994

I f you have ever thought that early American history was a little on the dry side, Elizabeth George Speare might change your mind. Her books capture the struggle of early Americans while telling a rip-roaring story. She wrote about settlers being captured by Native Americans and told stories about life in the colonies. One of her tales is about an orphaned girl sailing from Barbados to live with a relative in Connecticut. She becomes friends with a woman who is believed to be a witch—at a time when being a witch could bring the whole village carrying torches and calling for blood.

Elizabeth George was born in Melrose, Massachusetts, on November 21, 1908, the daughter of an architect, Harry Allan George, and his wife, Demetria. Elizabeth grew up in a typical New England setting and started writing at an

ELIZABETH GEORGE SPEARE RECEIVED THE NEWBERY MEDAL TWICE, IN 1959 FOR *THE WITCH OF BLACKBIRD POND* AND IN 1962 FOR *THE BRONZE BOW*.

early age. She took walks in the woods, picked blueberries, and traveled to the seaside during the summer. She could often be found reading and dreaming. She loved stories and began to write her own to pass the days.

She attended Boston University, where she earned a bachelor's degree and a master's degree. After she graduated, she wanted to share her love of stories with children, so she taught English in high schools.

> "I began to write from the age of eight on. I filled volumes of brown note-books with poetry and stories, all more incredibly naive than any child could write today."

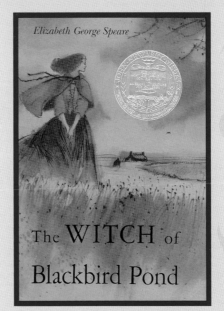

A Selected Bibliography of Speare's Work

The Sign of the Beaver (1983)
Ice Glen (1967)
The Prospering (1967)
Life in Colonial America (1963)
The Bronze Bow (1961)
The Witch of Blackbird Pond (1958)
Calico Captive (1957)

Speare's Major Literary Awards

1989 Laura Ingalls Wilder Award

1984 Newbery Honor Book
1984 Scott O'Dell Award
   The Sign of the Beaver

1962 Newbery Medal
   The Bronze Bow

1959 Newbery Medal
   The Witch of Blackbird Pond

In 1936, she married Alden Speare, an industrial engineer, and moved to Wethersfield, Connecticut. The couple had two children, Alden Jr. and Mary Elizabeth. While her children were young, Speare spent time at home. But she never lost her interest in stories.

Moving to Connecticut prompted Speare to start reading about the region. She began to write about Connecticut and its history. Her articles were published in various magazines, and one was adapted for television.

During her research, Speare discovered a diary from 1796 of a young woman who had been held captive by Native Americans. The 200-year-old book, *The Narrative of the Captivity of Mrs. Johnson,* prompted Speare to retell the story for young readers. The result, *Calico Captive,* brought out the personalities of two sisters captured by Native Americans after an evening party, while remaining true to the setting of the actual story. The book was praised for presenting historical fiction with a real pulse.

Speare chose her own town of Wethersfield as the setting for her next book, *The Witch of Blackbird Pond.* The characters were her own creation, but the

> *"[During the writing of the* **The Witch of Blackbird Pond,***] Kit Tyler and her imaginary family and friends came to seem very real to me, and when this book won the Newbery Medal in 1959, I was happy to know they had made so many friends for themselves."*

SPEARE LOVED THE HISTORICAL RESEARCH THAT ALLOWED HER TO WRITE HER HISTORICAL FICTION. SHE SAID THAT SHE COULD SPEND HOURS AND HOURS RESEARCHING ONE MINOR DETAIL OF A BOOK.

setting is New England in 1687, and Speare ferreted out all the records she could from the period and consulted local historians.

Speare's interest in early American history also led to her writing *Life in Colonial America,* a nonfiction book. But Elizabeth George Speare is best remembered for her ability to breathe life into history through the telling of gripping stories. She died on November 15, 1994.

&

WHERE TO FIND OUT MORE ABOUT ELIZABETH GEORGE SPEARE

BOOKS

Apseloff, Marilyn Fain. *Elizabeth George Speare.* New York: Twayne Publications, 1992.

Kovacs, Deborah, and James Preller. *Meet the Authors and Illustrators: 60 Creators of Favorite Children's Books Talk about Their Work.* Vol.1. New York: Scholastic, 1993.

McElmeel, Sharron L. *100 Most Popular Children's Authors: Biographical Sketches and Bibliographies.* Englewood, Colo.: Libraries Unlimited, 1999.

WEB SITES

CAROL HURST'S CHILDREN'S LITERATURE SITE
http://www.carolhurst.com/titles/signofthe.html
To read a review of *The Sign of the Beaver*

EDUCATIONAL PAPERBACK ASSOCIATION
http://edupaperback.org/showauth.cfm?authid=85
For more information about Speare's life and work

DURING THE LAST YEARS OF HER LIFE, SPEARE WORKED WITH RESEARCHERS AT THE UNIVERSITY OF CONNECTICUT TO HELP SIMPLIFY THE LIVES OF HANDICAPPED HOMEMAKERS.

Peter Spier

Born: June 6, 1927

Peter Spier has illustrated more than forty books that he wrote. He has also illustrated more than 150 books for other authors. Along the way, he has won a Caldecott Medal, the highest honor a children's book illustrator can earn. Spier's books include *Noah's Ark, The Fox Went Out on a Chilly Night: An Old Song, People,* and *Bored—Nothing to Do!*

Peter Spier was born on June 6, 1927, in Amsterdam, the Netherlands. He grew up in a town called Broek-in-Waterland. Another famous person who grew up in this town was Hans Brinker, the young boy who supposedly rescued his village from flooding by sticking his finger in a dike.

SPIER'S BOOKS HAVE BEEN TRANSLATED INTO TWENTY-FOUR LANGUAGES.

Peter and his brother and sister all went to school in the city of Amsterdam. They lived near the sea, and the family spent their weekends sailing. Peter enjoyed being on the water. As an adult, he still sails. He also builds model ships.

Peter's father was a journalist and political cartoonist. Peter watched his father work, and he began to draw, too. By the time he finished high school in 1945, he knew he wanted to be an artist, so he enrolled in a school to study art. Two years later, Spier had to serve in the Netherlands's navy. He traveled to the West Indies and South America.

> *"If you don't know what it looks like, don't draw it."*

Peter Spier left the navy in 1951 and got a job for the largest newspaper in the Netherlands. First he was assigned to work in Paris, France, and then in the United States. After working for awhile in Houston, Texas, Spier decided to move to New York and illustrate children's books.

The first book he illustrated was *Cocoa,* which was written by Margaret G. Otto. It was published in 1953. For the next eight years, Spier illustrated books for other authors. Then, in 1961, Spier illustrated a folk song in *The Fox Went Out on a Chilly Night: An Old Song.* It was instantly popular and was named a Caldecott Honor Book.

PETER SPIER BECAME A U.S. CITIZEN IN 1958.

A Selected Bibliography of Spier's Work

Father, May I Come? (1993)

The Book of Jonah (1985)

Trucks, Trucks, Trucks (Illustrations only, 1984)

Peter Spier's Rain (1982)

People (1980)

The Legend of New Amsterdam (1979)

Bored—Nothing to Do! (1978)

Noah's Ark (1977)

The Star-Spangled Banner (Illustrations only, 1973)

Tin Lizzie (1975)

The Erie Canal (1970)

London Bridge Is Falling Down! (1967)

To Market! To Market! (1967)

The Fox Went Out on a Chilly Night: An Old Song (1961)

The Cow Who Fell in the Canal (Illustrations only, 1957)

Cocoa (Illustrations only, 1953)

Spier's Major Literary Awards

1982 American Book Award
1978 Caldecott Medal
   Noah's Ark

1967 Boston Globe–Horn Book Picture Book Award
   London Bridge Is Falling Down!

1962 Caldecott Honor Book
   The Fox Went Out on a Chilly Night: An Old Song

Since then, many of Spier's books have won awards. He is known for his careful, detailed illustrations. In fact, some of his books have very few or no words. One of these books is *Noah's Ark,* which retells the well-known Bible story almost entirely in pictures. In his *Peter Spier's Rain,* Spier uses only pictures to tell the story of a brother and sister caught in a rainstorm.

"None of [the other retellings of the story] shows Noah shoveling manure or even hinted at the stench and the mess inside. It was then that I knew that there was room for one more Noah's Ark."

Children and adults enjoy Peter Spier's illustrations. They like the vitality and humor of his drawings. In the book entitled *People,* Spier drew fifty-four different noses on one page!

Spier continue to win awards, and some of his books have been made into videos. He lives with his wife in Shoreham, New York, where he continues to write and illustrate children's books. "As long as your hand is steady, you can keep on making books for as long as you wish. The wonderful thing for me is I don't *have* to do it anymore. I'm doing it because it's still fun," says Spier.

WHERE TO FIND OUT MORE ABOUT PETER SPIER

BOOKS

De Montveville, Dorris, and Donna Hill, eds. *Third Book of Junior Authors.*
New York: H. W. Wilson Company, 1972

Kovacs, Deborah, and James Preller. *Meet the Authors and Illustrators:*
60 Creators of Favorite Children's Books Talk about Their Work. Vol. 2.
New York: Scholastic, 1993.

WEB SITES

ENCYCLOPAEDIA BRITANNICA
http://www.britannica.com/ebi/article-9337111
To find biographical information about Spier.

MCCAIN LIBRARY AND ARCHIVES
http://www.lib.usm.edu/%7Edegrum/html/research/findaids/spier.htm
To find biographical information about Spier

SPIER CREATED THE MOTHER GOOSE LIBRARY SERIES IN 1967.
HE SELECTED, ADAPTED, AND ILLUSTRATED EACH BOOK IN THE SERIES.

Jerry Spinelli

Born: February 1, 1941

When kids ask Jerry Spinelli where he gets his ideas for his books, his answer is simple: "I get them from you. You're the funny ones." His humorous books for young people have made Spinelli an award-winning author. His best-known books for young people include *Maniac Magee, Space Station Seventh Grade,* and *There's a Girl in My Hammerlock.*

Spinelli was born on February 1, 1941, in Norristown, Pennsylvania. He did not spend much time reading or writing when he was young. Instead, he spent most of his time playing baseball. Jerry played on Little League teams as well as in junior and senior high school. He dreamed of being a major league baseball player.

SPINELLI'S FAVORITE BOOK OF HIS IS *MANIAC MAGEE.*
HE LIKES "THE MESSAGE, THE STORY, AND THE LANGUAGE."

Jerry did not think of becoming a writer until he was about sixteen years old. His high school's football team won a big game, and everyone was celebrating. Jerry had a different way to celebrate. He wrote a poem about the game, which was published in the local newspaper a few days later. Jerry quickly became interested in becoming a writer.

"Now I don't really write for adults or kids—I don't write for kids, I write about them. I think you need to do that, otherwise you end up preaching down. You need to listen not so much to the audience but to the story itself."

A Selected Bibliography of Spinelli's Work

Tooter Pepperday (2004)
Milkweed (2003)
My Daddy and Me (2003)
Loser (2002)
Stargirl (2000)
Knots in My Yo-Yo String: The Autobiography of a Kid (1998)
Wringer (1997)
Crash (1996)
Do the Funky Pickle (1992)
Fourth Grade Rats (1991)
School Daze: Report to the Principal's Office (1991)
There's a Girl in My Hammerlock (1991)
Maniac Magee (1990)
The Bathwater Gang (1990)
Dump Days (1988)
Jason and Marceline (1986)
Night of the Whale (1985)
Who Put That Hair in My Toothbrush? (1984)
Space Station Seventh Grade (1982)

Spinelli's Major Literary Awards

1998 Newbery Honor Book
    Wringer
1991 Newbery Medal
1990 Boston Globe-Horn Book Fiction Award
    Maniac Magee

After graduating from high school, Jerry Spinelli attended Gettysburg College and Johns Hopkins University. When he finished college, he took a job as an editor for a magazine. He also began writing novels for adults. Spinelli used his lunch breaks to write. He wrote four novels for adults but was not able to find anyone to publish them.

In 1977, Spinelli married Eileen Mesi, who is also a writer. Eileen already had six children, so Spinelli became an instant father.

Being the father to six children changed Spinelli's career as a writer. Spinelli found the inspiration for his first published book, *Space Station Seventh Grade,* by observing his own children. "For the first two books, I didn't even have to look outside my own house," Spinelli says.

> *"I like to let it be chaotic, so possibilities can reign and prevail. Out of that mess, gradually, hopefully, a story will begin to take shape."*

Spinelli also gets ideas for his books from his memories of growing up in a small town. "I thought I was simply growing up in Norristown, Pennsylvania," Spinelli notes. "Looking back now I can see that I was also gathering material that would one day find its way into my books." Spinelli uses humor to tell his stories. He has tackled tough topics such as racism, bullying, and sex.

THE INSPIRATION FOR SPINELLI'S *THERE'S A GIRL IN MY HAMMERLOCK* CAME FROM A NEWSPAPER STORY HE READ ABOUT A GIRL WHO COMPETED ON HER HIGH SCHOOL WRESTLING TEAM.

Spinelli has written more than twenty books for young readers.

He lives with his family in Pennsylvania, where he continues to write.

❧

WHERE TO FIND OUT MORE ABOUT JERRY SPINELLI

BOOKS

Kovacs, Deborah, and James Preller. *Meet the Authors and Illustrators: 60 Creators of Favorite Children's Books Talk about Their Work.* Vol. 2. New York: Scholastic, 1993.

McElmeel, Sharron L. *100 Most Popular Children's Authors: Biographical Sketches and Bibliographies.* Englewood, Colo.: Libraries Unlimited, 1999.

McGinty, Alice B. *Meet Jerry Spinelli.* New York: PowerKids Press, 2003.

Spinelli, Jerry. *In My Own Words.* New York: Simon and Schuster, 1997.

Spinelli, Jerry. *Knots in My Yo-Yo String. The Autobiography of a Kid.* New York: Knopf, 1998.

WEB SITES

EDUCATIONAL PAPERBACK ASSOCIATION
http://edupaperback.org/showauth.cfm?authid=74
To learn more about Spinelli's work

JERRY SPINELLI HOME PAGE
http://www.jerryspinelli.com/newbery_001.htm
For information about the author and his works

HOUGHTON MIFFLIN MEET THE AUTHOR
http://www.eduplace.com/kids/hmr/mtai/spinelli.html
To read about Jerry Spinelli's life and books

———

SPINELLI BECAME A CHILDREN'S BOOK AUTHOR BY ACCIDENT. PUBLISHERS OF ADULT BOOKS WERE NOT INTERESTED IN *SPACE STATION SEVENTH GRADE* BECAUSE IT WAS ABOUT A THIRTEEN-YEAR-OLD. THEN A CHILDREN'S BOOK PUBLISHER LIKED THE BOOK AND PUBLISHED IT.

Diane Stanley

Born: December 27, 1943

ost of Diane Stanley's picture books are nonfiction. Sometimes they use beautiful, detailed illustrations to help tell the stories of people from history. Her best-known books include *Leonardo da Vinci, Cleopatra,* and *Peter the Great.*

Diane Stanley was born on December 27, 1943, in Abilene, Texas. Diane's parents divorced when she was very young. She lived in New York with her mother, Fay, who was an important part of her life. In fact, Diane Stanley believes it is because of her mother that she is an author today.

Fay Stanley took her daughter to museums and to the theater, and they read many books together. Fay Stanley even helped Diane write her first book! "She would type up my words, and I would draw the

---

SOME OF STANLEY'S BOOKS WERE PUBLISHED UNDER
THE NAME DIANE ZUROMSKIS.

144

pictures," remembers Stanley. Fay Stanley herself wrote mystery books. From her mother's efforts, Diane saw that ordinary people could be successful authors if they liked words and worked hard.

Fay Stanley became very ill at one point, so Diane was sent back to Abilene to live with her aunt and uncle for several years. Then, she and her mother moved to La Jolla, California. When her mother became ill again, Diane returned to Texas and finished high school there.

After high school, Stanley attended Trinity University in San Antonio, Texas. She was interested in many things in college, including history and politics. But during her last year in college, she took an art course. "The teacher took me aside and told me he thought I had ability. That teacher changed the course of my life," notes Stanley. "I wonder how many teachers realize the power they have to mold the lives of their students?"

"Today, my life is all about books: writing them, illustrating them, reading them, and sharing them with children. I feel blessed."

Then, Diane Stanley went to Johns Hopkins University, where she earned a master's degree in medical illustration. In 1970, she married and started work as a medical illustrator. She soon had two daughters.

Stanley read to her children as her mother had read to her. It was during this time that Stanley decided to write children's books. "I realized

---

STANLEY ILLUSTRATED A BOOK WRITTEN BY HER MOTHER. THE BOOK IS *THE LAST PRINCESS: THE STORY OF PRINCESS KA'IULANI OF HAWAI'I.*

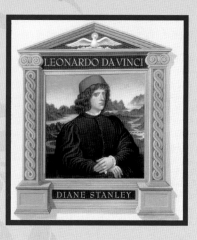

A Selected Bibliography of Stanley's Work

Bella at Midnight: the Thimble, the Ring and the Slipper of Glass (2006)

Thanksgiving on Plymouth Plantation (2004)

Saladin: Noble Prince of Islam (2002)

Michaelangelo (2001)

Peter the Great (1999)

Joan of Arc (1998)

Saving Sweetness (Text only, 1996)

Leonardo da Vinci (1996)

The True Adventure of Daniel Hall (1995)

Cleopatra (with Peter Vennema, 1994)

Charles Dickens: The Man Who Had Great Expectations (with Peter Vennema, 1993)

Moe the Dog in Tropical Paradise (1992)

The Last Princess: The Story of Princess Ka'iulani of Hawai'i (Illustrations only, 1991)

Good Queen Bess: The Story of Elizabeth I of England (with Peter Vennema, 1990)

Shaka: King of the Zulus (with Peter Vennema, 1988)

The Conversation Club (1983)

The Farmer in the Dell (Illustrations only, 1978)

Stanley's Major Literary Awards

2001 Orbis Pictus Honor Book
  Michaelangelo

1997 Boston Globe-Horn Book Nonfiction Honor Book
1997 Orbis Pictus Award
  Leonardo da Vinci

1992 Carter G. Woodson Book Award
  The Last Princess: The Story of Princess Ka'iulani of Hawai'i

1991 Boston Globe-Horn Book Nonfiction Honor Book
  Good Queen Bess: The Story of Elizabeth I of England

that what I really wanted to do was make books for children. It was the perfect combination of my love of words, art, and book design," says Stanley.

Diane Stanley carefully researches a topic before she begins to write. She reads hundreds of pages before she begins writing and illustrating. Stanley often writes about people in history and events that happened in faraway places. Stanley likes to travel to see the places for herself so she can add details to both the story and the pictures. Sometimes she researches the pictures as much as she does the story.

Stanley and her second husband, Peter Vennema, live in Houston, Texas, where she continues to write and illustrate books for children. "I have deeply enjoyed moving along the path I set out upon over twenty years ago. Part of the fun is not knowing where it will take me," Stanley explains.

> *"If the reader doesn't have a feeling for the world my subject lived in, the story won't really come to life."*

WHERE TO FIND OUT MORE ABOUT DIANE STANLEY

BOOKS

Holtze, Sally Holmes, ed. *Sixth Book of Junior Authors & Illustrators.* New York: H .W. Wilson Company, 1989.

McElmeel, Sharron L. *100 Most Popular Picture Book Authors and Illustrators: Biographical Sketches and Bibliographies.* Englewood, Colo.: Libraries Unlimited, 2000.

WEB SITES

CHILDREN'S BOOK COUNCIL
http://www.cbcbooks.org/cbcmagazine/meet/dianestanley.html
To learn what Stanley says about her work

DIANE STANLEY'S HOME PAGE
http://www.dianestanley.com/
For information about Stanley's life and books

STANLEY AND HER HUSBAND, PETER VENNEMA, HAVE WORKED TOGETHER ON SEVERAL BOOKS.

Suzanne Fisher Staples

Born: August 27, 1945

Few people have seen the world as Suzanne Fisher Staples has. As an international news reporter, she has lived in a wide variety of countries. She draws on her foreign experiences in writing her young adult novels. Several of her books are set in exotic locations where readers explore unfamiliar cultures from an insider's point of view.

Suzanne Fisher was born in Philadelphia, Pennsylvania, in 1945. The

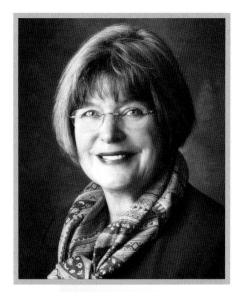

family home was in a small, lakeside community in northeastern Pennsylvania. Suzanne grew up there with her sister and two brothers.

As a child, Suzanne wrote poetry, kept a diary, and even started a newspaper. She loved reading stories on many subjects, too. Books opened her mind up to experiences and adventures outside her own world. She recalls that she was a "terrible daydreamer."

A TIGER ATTACKED AN ELEPHANT THAT STAPLES WAS RIDING DURING A TRIP TO INDIA. SHE TURNED THIS EXPERIENCE INTO A SCENE IN *SHIVA'S FIRE*.

"My books are made up of real stories about real people."

She attended Cedar Crest College in Allentown, Pennsylvania, graduating in 1967. Her areas of special study were English literature and political science. These subjects provided a great background for her future work.

She joined United Press International as a news reporter and editor in 1975. As a foreign correspondent, she worked in Hong Kong, India, Pakistan, Afghanistan, Bangladesh, Nepal, and Sri Lanka. Living in these locations, she acquired a deep understanding of foreign cultures. While in Pakistan, she met a teacher named Eugene Staples. They were married in 1980, though the marriage later ended in divorce.

In 1983, Suzanne Fisher Staples moved to Washington, D.C., where she became a foreign news editor for the *Washington Post* newspaper. During this time, she began thinking seriously

"I have been concerned for some time about Americans' understanding of foreign nations and peoples."

about writing a book. Looking over her notebooks, she started writing down scenes that came to mind as she recalled her experiences.

In 1985, the U.S. Agency for International Development sent Staples to Pakistan to study the lives of poor women in rural areas. She spent three years with nomadic people in Pakistan's Cholistan Desert, learning

---

SUZANNE'S FAVORITE CHILDHOOD BOOKS INCLUDED *BLACK BEAUTY* BY ANNA SEWELL AND *THE YEARLING* BY MARJORIE KINNAN RAWLINGS.

A Selected Bibliography of Staples's Work

Under the Persimmon Tree (2005)
The Green Dog: A Mostly True Story (2003)
Shiva's Fire (2000)
Dangerous Skies (1996)
Haveli (1993)
Shabanu: Daughter of the Wind (1989)

Staples's Major Literary Awards

1990 Newbery Honor Book
  Shabanu: Daughter of the Wind

about their daily lives, as well as their deep religious devotion as Muslims. This experience became the basis for her first published book.

Staples's novel *Shabanu: Daughter of the Wind* was published in 1989. It's about a young Pakistani girl who must enter an arranged marriage to preserve her family's honor. This book gives the reader an inside glimpse into the world of Pakistan's nomadic camel herders. Its sequel, *Haveli*, explores the same girl's struggles with married life.

In *Shiva's Fire*, Staples tells of a young girl in India who becomes a dancer with magical powers. To research this book, Staples journeyed back to India. There she observed dance students and learned the principles and legends of India's Hindu religion. *Under the Persimmon Tree* grew out of Staples's experiences in Afghanistan. It's about a young Afghan girl who is full of hope in spite of the upheavals in her war-torn country.

Staples used her own childhood memories for *The Green Dog: A Mostly True Story*. It's the heartwarming tale of a girl and her beloved dog. The two spend their long summer days exploring the woods and waterways of northeastern Pennsylvania.

Staples continues writing from her home in Chattanooga, Tennessee.

❧

WHERE TO FIND OUT MORE ABOUT SUZANNE FISHER STAPLES

BOOK

Holtze, Sally Holmes. *Seventh Book of Junior Authors and Illustrators.*
New York: H. W. Wilson, 1996.

WEB SITES

CHILDREN'S BOOK PAGE
http://www.bookpage.com/0508bp/children/under_the_persimmon_tree.html
For an interview of the author by Alice Cary

SUZANNE FISHER STAPLES HOME PAGE
http://www.suzannefisherstaples.com/
For a listing of her books, interviews, questions, and a biography

WALKER BOOKS
http://www.walkerbooks.co.uk/Suzanne-Fisher-Staples
For an autobiography and a list of things you don't know about her

———

STAPLES SPENDS ABOUT FOUR TO FIVE HOURS A DAY WRITING.
WHEN SHE GETS STUCK, SHE SOMETIMES WANDERS IN THE WOODS WITH A
NOTEPAD TO GET IDEAS FLOWING AGAIN.

William Steig

Born: November 14, 1907
Died: October 3, 2003

As a young man, William Steig (pictured with his wife) wanted to go to sea—to set sail for unknown lands in search of adventure. Many children dream of traveling to magical lands where they meet strange creatures. Steig never did go to sea. Instead, through his writing he launched more than thirty expeditions into the world of the imagination. His ships were his books, and his building materials were pictures and words. His books are filled with strange, sometimes ugly creatures made likable through their charm and goodness. They have sailed into the homes of children all over the world.

William Steig was familiar with painting from a young age. Born on November 14, 1907, in New York City, he had two parents who loved to paint. His father, Joseph, who

WILLIAM STEIG DIDN'T START WRITING FOR CHILDREN UNTIL HE WAS IN HIS SIXTIES, WHEN MOST ADULTS ARE THINKING ABOUT RETIREMENT.

was originally from Austria, worked as a housepainter to support the family. In his spare time, he joined his wife, Laura, at the easel, where the two painted for pleasure. William's brother Irwin became a professional painter. It was Irwin Steig who first gave William lessons on how to work colors on a palette and dab them on a canvas until the picture took on a life of its own.

In 1923, William Steig enrolled in the City College of New York. After graduating,

"Art, including juvenile literature, has the power to make any spot on earth the living center of the universe."

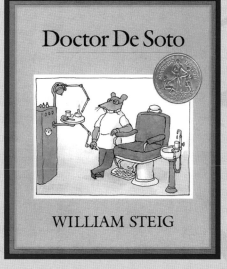

A Selected Bibliography of Steig's Work

When Everybody Wore a Hat (2003)
Potch & Polly (2001)
Wizzil (2000)
Gift from Zeus: Sixteen Favorite Myths (Illustrations only, 2001)
Grown-Ups Get to Do All the Driving (1995)
Shrek! (1990)
Spinky Sulks (1988)
Doctor De Soto (1982)
Tiffky Doofky (1978)
Caleb & Kate (1977)
Abel's Island (1976)
The Amazing Bone (1976)
Dominic (1972)
Amos & Boris (1971)
Sylvester and the Magic Pebble (1969)
C D B (1968)

Steig's Major Literary Awards

1983 Boston Globe-Horn Book Picture Book Honor Book
1983 Newbery Honor Book
1982 American Book Award
Doctor De Soto

1977 Boston Globe-Horn Book Picture Book Honor Book
1977 Caldecott Honor Book
The Amazing Bone

1977 Newbery Honor Book
Abel's Island

1970 Caldecott Medal
Sylvester and the Magic Pebble

Steig sought professional art training at the National Academy of Design in New York City. Manhattan in the 1920s was a sea of dark-suited businessmen in dark hats. It was also a place filled with immigrants, who hoped to get rich in America. In short, it was a paradise for people who loved to watch people.

> *"I have a position—a point of view. But I don't have to think about it to express it. I can write about anything and my point of view will come out."*

Steig began to read the private struggles of these people on their faces. He observed the funny, sometimes absurd side of normal, everyday folks. He transformed these observations into cartoon drawings. He sold one of these cartoons to the *New Yorker,* a witty, intellectual New York magazine with a tradition of excellent cartoons. During his career, he contributed hundreds of cartoons to the magazine.

After almost forty years as a successful cartoonist, William Steig decided to try something new. He turned to children's fiction and illustration. His sense of comedy was transformed into adventure tales for children.

Steig's characters are pigs and mice who are often quite witty. They live in a world that feels safe, despite the presence of danger. Characters such as Shrek, a hideous green monster, are likable because they are

IN 2001, STEIG'S POPULAR BOOK *SHREK!* WAS TURNED INTO AN ANIMATED MOVIE THAT BECAME POPULAR WITH CHILDREN AND ADULTS.

funny and loyal to their friends. The lumpy Shrek is like an excitable version of sleepy Winnie-the-Pooh, and he captures the same innocent goodness. Over the years, Steig created characters who found a vast audience of children hungry for intelligent entertainment. He died on October 3, 2003, in his Boston home.

❧

WHERE TO FIND OUT MORE ABOUT WILLIAM STEIG

BOOKS

Chevalier, Tracy, ed. *Twentieth-Century Children's Writers.* 3rd ed. Chicago: St. James Press, 1989.

Kovacs, Deborah, and James Preller. *Meet the Authors and Illustrators: 60 Creators of Favorite Children's Books Talk about Their Work.* Vol. 1. New York: Scholastic, 1991.

Lorenz, Lee, ed. *The World of William Steig.* New York: Artisan, 1998.

Rockman, Connie C., ed. *The Ninth Book of Junior Authors and Illustrators.* New York: H. W. Wilson Company, 2004.

WEB SITES

KIDSREADS.COM
http://www.kidsreads.com/authors/au-steig-william.asp
For a biography of William Steig and related links

WILLIAM STEIG'S HOME PAGE
http://www.williamsteig.com/
For a lot of information about William Steig

WILLIAM STEIG PUBLISHED MORE THAN 1,600 CARTOONS IN THE *NEW YORKER* AND DESIGNED 117 CARTOON COVERS FOR THE MAGAZINE.

INDEX